The Story of Glory

The Story of Glory

By
Lori Willey

The Story of Glory

Published by Lori Willey
10216 Clinton Ave. S.
Bloomington, MN

Cover design by Dugan Design Group
Interior design by Bethany Press International
Printed by Bethany Press International

ISBN: 978-0-578-09257-7

Dedication

To Mom and Dad

"Train up a child in the way he should go and when he is old he will not turn from it." Proverbs 22:6, NIV

Thank you, Alan, for your support in getting our story told.

Chapter 1
Dreams

"Sweet sixteen and never been kissed." It was the summer of my sixteenth year. I had longed for a boyfriend—that first kiss and the attention of my Cinderella's-dream prince. The purpose of being a teenager, in my mind, was to find the man of my dreams and have him fall head-over-heels in love with me.

I imagined my prince to be completely in love with me. He would be jealous for my attentions. He would protect me from other's advances. He would be strong and carry me in his arms in play and romance. He would be thoughtful and always there for me and would never want to leave me. He would provide for me, laugh with me, and comfort me. We would do everything together for the rest of our lives.

Most of my social time with boys happened at church. Some were friends with whom I had fun, but never noticed their interest in me. Other boys I would notice and did everything I could to get their attention. I would wear the latest clothing fashions and do my hair just right. I attempted to be feminine, silly, and sweet.

Finally, after great effort for months on end doing my curling iron just right for the perfect hair flip, one of the good-looking and *older* church boys—a senior in high school—asked me for a date. Victory! My dreams had come true! This was it! I was going to be looking good on his arm. I liked his parents. *Great in-*

laws, I thought to myself as I made up my future. It was perfect. We would marry in our church. We even had the same friends. I couldn't wait until he picked me up for our first date.

He arrived in an older brother's car. He barely got to come to the door as I darted out, ready to go. I'd spent hours getting ready. Every item of clothing was chosen carefully. My hair was perfect. My comb was readily accessible in my back pocket in case any wisp of hair got out of place. Walking swiftly across a summer's lawn of green grass, I settled into my carriage. *Silence*. I barely spoke. The funny, flirty, and friendly girl clammed up and turned into church mouse. Educated by my *Teen Heartbeat* magazines, I was allowing him to talk about himself. The problem was he didn't talk much either. The gaps of silence, my wonder and nervousness, were painful to me. I never thought he too, may be noticing the silence, so I never interjected anything.

At the end of the date he lunged at me. I don't remember words before the lunging. It was my first kiss. Maybe his silence was plotting. He kissed me long and strong. I definitely wasn't doing things right. My teeth were hurting the inside of my mouth. By the time it was done I felt like I'd been hit with a baseball. Not knowing any better, I thought this was a good night. The prize was a boyfriend, a kiss and a happily ever after—despite puffy lips.

Days started to pass and he didn't call. Sunday came and I knew I would see him at church. He side-stepped me or looked down whenever I was close. Something was up. Even my imagination-filled, 16-year-old, perfectly-coiffed- head knew that.

There was a professional soccer game coming up. It was the Minnesota Kicks. My neglectful prince worked in the stands selling t-shirts at these games. These events and games were enormously popular. We are talking 30,000-50,000 fans in attendance. Parking was free and tickets were cheap. It was the invasion of attractive-legged players from all over the world; our first global experience in our otherwise bland suburbia of the late 1970's. Fireworks shows followed home games. Explosives were shot for goals made. Famous bands played concerts after some of the games. It was an event, and you weren't cool unless you went.

I walked the concourses until I found his t-shirt sales stand. People were pressing and swarming as they socialized and looked for their gate entrances, while buying treats or t-shirts. He was busy at his stand, but that didn't stop me from pushing my way through.

"Why haven't you called me?" For goodness sakes, he'd practically kissed my face off. He went flush as he looked up and saw it was me. He stammered a little, but pretty much said he didn't like me anymore. I burst into tears and through my sobs—which were quite loud—bawled, "No one will ever date me again!" In panic and terror, he looked over to the other guy who was selling shirts. His co-worker quickly looked away and actually walked to the furthest end of the table, which left my new "ex" to deal with me. He faced the problem, stepping closer to me and saying with sincere sympathy and compassion, "You will date again, you will." I staggered away through the crowd with my face in my hands and cried for the duration of the game. My glass slipper was shattered.

Little did I know that in seven years, I would marry the star soccer player from England who was playing on that field in front of all of those thousands of screaming fans and a sobbing me.

I did date again. I dated a lot. I dated carelessly, competitively, seriously, vulnerably, aggressively, hopefully, and hopelessly. I was making my own nightmare. What had been a beautiful dream turned into darkness. High school had continued youthful mistakes and misunderstandings...and just plain stupidity.

Hoping to still land a "good guy" from church, I remained selective in that area while dabbling with the bad guys. Some of the good guys who adored me, I didn't adore back. I just wanted someone to like me as much as I liked them. It was a constant search.

College came and the darkness thickened. I began partying. Alcohol was the guest at most of my social gatherings. What I thought was fun and good times brought me to regrets and more heartache. A relationship that I did value crumbled as he pointed out that my "priorities were different than his." His were on a straighter and more promising road. Mine zigzagged from party to party. What should have sobered me up brought me down harder. I became colder and more reckless and lost.

Dropping out of college, I moved back to the city. I got a job at one of the newest and trendiest hot spots as a hostess. This brought the party scene from social to now being my job.

It brought my dating to a frenzied pace. It was insanity. I was finding a high in how many men I could have chasing me. Because of where I worked, I came into contact with a lot of the people on the local scene. I dated businessmen, professional football and hockey players, waiters, musicians; a pro-wrestler was even after me, you name it. Some I dumped, some dumped me; the whole time wanting to find *The One*. I had become very outgoing. People liked to be around me. But inside, I wanted a husband, someone with whom to share my life.

A girlfriend and I went to the Christmas Eve candlelight service at my church. I was dressed more like I was ready for a nightclub. I remember clearly how we stood in the lobby and looked for people we knew from our high school days. I remember a feeling of separation. It was powerful because the memory is still so clear. After the service, one of the businessmen I knew called and asked if we wanted to meet for an after-midnight breakfast at a 24-hour pancake place. We did. The waitress said, "Merry Christmas." I had a pang that shot in my heart. My girlfriend left the restaurant earlier and drove home to bed before me. After hanging around pretty long he ended up sending me home in a cab so he wouldn't have to give me a ride back. He was probably more interested in my friend. The sting of what was supposed to be—and had previously been—a beautiful night celebrating my Savior's birth was dark and empty and lonely.

In a haze of numbness, darkness, and self-destructive ways, the memory of that night is so clear. Now as I look back, I see that it must be clarity of the light that God was trying to shine for me to show clearly where I was—away from Him. As much as I was alone, Jesus was there and trying to make me notice. Foolishly, selfishly, I neglected it and Him.

Another memory was jolted back recently of those days and again with great clarity. I recently attended a day-long event called "SOZO." It is based on the Hebrew word used to mean healing and deliverance. The leader started the day with an "ice breaker" for those seated together at a table. We'd just had a big December snowfall the night before, so his questions were, "What snowfall impacted you the most and what is your favorite Christmas carol?" While being in the midst of writing this, I recalled the memory.

I shared with the timid group first. The snowfall happened a month after the Christmas I described. It was another night holed up in a bar with a girlfriend. As we partied with the usual crowd and drank our drink specials, the snow was falling heavily. We paid no mind to it. As the evening went on, the bartender got a phone call from the manager of the motel next door. They must have noticed the cars parked outside the establishment, knew there was drinking and terrible conditions, and they offered everyone in the bar a free room for the night. He announced it and we all cheered and drank more.

The next morning reality and sobriety hit. We were dressed in clubbing clothes, no shovel, and a parking lot and car covered in eight inches of snow. I called my parents who lived nearby, and asked for help or a shovel. I told them where I was—not that I shared how much I drank the night before—and they flatly said, "No." I was left to my own devices.

I was forced to go out into that snow, head throbbing and stomach sick from the drinking I did the night before. On hands and knees, I dug and scraped away the snow. The sky was crystal blue and the snow blinding white, and I dealt with what I allowed myself to be buried in. Struggling and slipping, feet and fingers numb, and with a hangover, I got my car out. The table leader said, "That's quite a metaphor." Then I answered the favorite Christmas carol question....

"O, Holy Night." They all laughed. Once again, God showed me He was there in the depth of my sin and the forgiveness coming, made white as snow. "Come now, let us reason together," says the LORD. "Though your sins are like scarlet, they shall be as white as snow; though they are red as crimson, they shall be like wool" (Isaiah 1:18, NIV).

Following that Christmas Eve, I didn't even try to go to church again until Easter. But as the life I was living stepped in, when I tried to get to church, I wasn't able to get there. I woke up Easter morning, got dressed and ready and walked out to my car. Its tires were flat. One of the guys who I had told I didn't want to date anymore came in the night and slashed my car tires with a knife. I called my brother for help and he came. I don't remember what he did or how anything got resolved, I just remember he came to help. I don't know why I didn't call my parents—maybe because I was too ashamed or knew they were on their way to church or that they didn't help in the blizzard. But, my brother came and it was a comfort.

CHAPTER 2

The Meeting

Months moved on and it was another summer night. My girlfriend and I went out to one of our usual hot spots. We skipped the peanut bar and headed downstairs to the nightclub. The live band was in full swing, the place was packed as it always was that particular night of the week. Every seat and booth were taken, people stood four-or-five deep watching a full dance floor. The bar was equally busy as the place swelled with cigarette smoke and warm bodies.

We made our way around the room of flashing lights, beating music, and conversations over the top of it, checking it all out to see who was there. It was easy to bump into friends from high school and on up. The bartender knew us and knew our drinks as he offered our favorite drinks out to us over the tops of the heads of the people in front of us. We drank, laughed, and talked to anyone who talked to us.

This night I leaned against the bar and talked with a funny, curly-haired guy from England. I had him laughing as much as he had me laughing. A friend of mine from high school pressed up behind me and whispered in my ear, "Lori, you know who you are talking to, don't you?" I brushed him off and said, "Yeah, yeah." I knew some of the pro soccer players were there that night. I figured he was maybe one from that bunch.

The team that had been such a huge phenomenon in the past had folded, and those players were scattered across the globe again. A new team was formed under the ownership of the people who owned the Miami Dolphins. I hadn't attended any of these games yet. They were at the new indoor football dome. Nothing seemed like a big deal to me and this particular guy didn't act like any of the "stars" I was used to seeing.

He wasn't egotistical, and didn't brag about himself or about anything he had or did. We didn't even exchange names or numbers. We just talked, joked, and laughed. I even dropped my chewed gum into his beer and laughed as he unknowingly took a gulp. He looked at me in disbelief, laughed, and was sickened all at the same time. It just made me laugh harder. In response, he pretended to give me a head butt, a soccer move to strike an air ball with the head since hands are not allowed. I found his response so funny and hadn't had anyone do that to me.

The evening flew by. My girlfriend found me and she and I walked off together and danced to a few of our favorite songs on the dance floor. As it became closing time, the last call was made, the lights came on and everyone headed to the stairs to go up and out to the parking lot.

It was always the slowest and dullest and most disappointing part of the night as the music stopped and we herded our way up the stairs. This time, as my girlfriend and I were going up, I noticed the guy I'd been goofing around with earlier. He was right in front of us on the stairs. In keeping with too many drinks and joking around, I looked up, saw his athletic bum and thought to myself, *This will be so funny. My friend will think this is hilarious, plus I'll never see him again.* I reached up and pinched that bum. He jumped so high and whipped his head around to see who did it while we burst out laughing. He faced forward again and kept on going. We reached the top and my girlfriend and I went out the door to my car and drove home.

The next day I worked during the lunch shift. I was working at the door greeting and seating people. The popularity of the place was still strong and it remained busy. One of my friends was working the door with me that day. As people streamed in and we were filling out our wait list, two guys came in and walked over to her. As I glanced up one of the guys looked over at me, pointed at me, leaned in, and said, "It was you!"

There was that curly-haired Englishman whose bum I had pinched the night before—and he was pointing at me! My mouth dropped open and my eyes got huge as I recognized him in disbelief. My friend walked over to me with the other fellow. She introduced me to them. She was dating his friend and they came in together for lunch to see her. We laughed a little and they asked if we wanted to meet them that evening for drinks. I didn't know for sure if I would make it. I wanted to, but I had a dinner date with one of the waiters. I thought maybe I could meet up with them afterward.

The fellow with whom I was to have a dinner date had been so kindhearted and brokenhearted, that I felt sorry for him and had said, "yes" to dinner. I recently had attended his mother's funeral. I was one of few friends who came.

It was a service unlike anything I had attended before. A woman had led the service. She spoke of Mother Earth, the wind, sky, and land. It was so odd and I felt sad that the Lord was not mentioned.

Things weren't sitting right within me. I don't know what the religion was called and I did not know there was anything like that even out there. Even in my lifestyle away from the Lord, I felt this wasn't right.

The night of our date he took me to a really nice restaurant and treated me so well. I had escargot for the first time, but all I could do was think about meeting up with my friend and those British fellows. I rushed through the evening and told him I was ready to go home and thanked him for a very nice dinner. I could tell he was disappointed and read that I was not interested in him any further than a friend.

Once home, I quickly got in my car and headed to join the others. That night was even more fun than the night before. We exchanged numbers this time. He called me the next day. We made more plans to get together. He would stop over at my apartment and he visited me at work. I loved it! I found out he was Alan Willey, one of the top goal scorers and stars of the amazing outdoor team. He had returned from playing in Canada and was playing for the newly formed team that played in the downtown Metrodome.

He did not resemble the super star I remembered from the previous outdoor team. His hair wasn't as puffy and it was brown. Before I'd thought he was a redhead under the lights and with the old team's orange jerseys. I'd never put that Alan together with the one I was dating until dates later, after having heard so many strangers go up to him and "know" him with a "Hi, Alan" or an autograph request.

Amazingly, I never went out with another man again. He was the only one I wanted to be with. He was fun, attentive, generous, and he seemed to adore me. I was thrilled to be falling in love with this star, and he was falling in love with me.

I knew this was going somewhere fast. I told my parents about him in a G-rated fairytale version. Fairytale is another word for a lie with prince and princess tendencies. I could never tell my saintly parents who'd raised me with godly values, prayers, and scriptures that I had pinched his bum after a night of drinking at a nightclub and that we ran into each other the next day through mutual friends. Oh no, I told a tale of meeting through mutual friends, of walking around a lake holding hands while others clued me in that it was ***The*** Alan Willey. I even proudly presented them with the Player Picture card of him that he'd autographed endearingly to me.

He treated my parents well and my friends. Everyone who met him thought he was witty and funny, and they were amazed at how down to earth he was. After three short months of dating, we began to talk about marriage. A total of five months after our first date, he bought a ring and a new sports car. As we sat in that new car in the middle of a shopping mall parking lot where he'd just walked across with the ring in a small jeweler's bag, he put that ring on my finger. We were engaged to be married. My dream was coming true. I was going to have a husband!

Quickly, the pride filled my eagerly-waiting frame. I felt important. Through his fame, everything seemed to be suddenly gilded. We were invited to sit in the best seats at events, restaurant owners gave us free dinners because we ate there and they wanted to encourage him to come back again. Airlines bumped us up to first class. Everyone wanted his business. A few took advantage of his business, too.

He did television interviews and radio shows, and newspaper reporters were always calling. He did team promotions by autograph sessions, celebrity golf tournaments, celebrity bartending, soccer demonstrations and exhibitions in and out of schools, attended charity events as a Celebrity Name draw, you name it. He had a top-name athletic wear contract and wore their brand for them. I remember a catalog coming and he told me to pick out whatever I wanted of the athletic wear, too. I attended almost everything he did, beaming.

It was a fantasy life; one he earned and one I eagerly joined. The limelight was blinding. It was hard to see what was in front of you. The inevitable end and the future without fame come for most all athletes. When you are in it, you are scarcely able to see what may come next—or anything else for that matter— unless the light within you is brighter than the limelight.

Chapter 3

He's the One

Opening up more about his life as we grew to know one another, trust one another, and listen to one another, he shared. Most all of his life was centered on soccer. It was what drove him and consumed him and brought him to this place.

As a very young child, he would get an orange in his Christmas stocking. He would kick the orange around his house until it was juice held in by its own skin. He would later poke a hole into the skin and suck out the juice to quench his thirst from the intensity of the play.

He was the oldest of five children growing up in Houghton Le Spring, England in a Counsel House. It was government subsidized housing, and nearly more common than not in that part of northeast England.

At the age of six, he came down with spinal meningitis. He was hospitalized for weeks. In the early 1960s when a child had such an illness, if it didn't kill them it nearly always left them paralyzed. Alan was blessed. He became well and whole again. His most traumatic memory of the illness was the injections, but mostly it was when he was dismissed from the hospital. His family had moved to another house while he was in the hospital. Coming home did not feel like home. He still speaks of it today.

He was a smart student, excelling in all classes with the exception of "Religious Knowledge." He had no interest and he was seated near the window that looked out over the soccer fields where his eyes would turn as he yearned to be there playing. He laughed as he shared that Religious Knowledge was his worse area of study, and my heart pained a little.

With not much money and many mouths to feed, he said he had to wear his father's shoes to school and that he came home with them beat, scuffed, and filthy as he continued to carry on with any game of soccer he could find. He remembered getting in trouble for it, but the lure of the game was greater.

He was a gifted athlete, one who did well above the rest. He was successful in cricket too, but soccer was his passion. Coaches in the local area began to notice him. He played in age groups higher than his own age as he matched them by his outstanding abilities. The adults took kindly to him. The nation's sport brought admiration to one who had such skills. Alan was polite and a hard worker. He was placed in areas of leadership in school and on the field. Although terribly shy, he rarely ventured to start a conversation. People seemed to come to him. The exception to Alan's shyness was his passion to get himself into a match. That is where the shyness fell away and the drive took over.

He told me his parents would drop him off for Sunday school and they would give him offering money. When they drove away, he would go purchase candies with his money and walk to where the men were playing soccer and he would watch or play. Laughingly, he said his parents would say he was the only child who could come out of Sunday school dirty.

Every now and then the children would recite a memory verse before the congregation. His parents would attend church the days of the children's recital. He made sure to go to Sunday school to get his memory verse, then cram for the day he was to recite it. He did what he needed to do and yet maintained his first passion, the sport.

He grew older and his skills excelled in the game. As success continued to come to him in soccer, he was noticed by a professional manager of the Middlesborough team. Alan signed professionally at the age of 17. At that time he was the youngest player ever to be signed to a professional contract in England.

School ended for children in England at the age of 16 and they had the option for two more years of further studies. Alan had completed an extra year and was ready and eager to earn a living at what he loved. He left home and moved to Middlesborough. His contract started him as an apprentice where he was housed with other apprentices.

Work as a professional athlete in an apprenticeship was more than playing the game of soccer. Alan told of times he had to sweep out the massive stadium stands with the other apprentices following the games. They aerated the fields literally foot by foot in cleated soccer shoes—or boots as they call them in England—and were instructed by a fastidious groundskeeper. If you have seen photos of English gardens, lawns, or stadium fields, you will notice the degree of perfection that is expected and undertaken. It was hard work added to what was exhausting training with the teams and playing the games.

The apprentices were even called in to work for the manager/owners in their leisure of hunting. The apprentices were to scare up the birds as they walked across rain, dew, or fog-soaked open fields; then ducking as those they were in contract for blasted away.

Alan never has had an interest in hunting. I can see where that has come from as well as his fear of guns.

Once recognized after having made multiple goals in important games, he was brought into high rankings and no longer had to work in the hardships of apprenticeship. He played hard. He did well. People noticed his skills. He did a lot of traveling. Traveling was something he didn't grow up with and something he'd never really thought about so it wasn't a priority. His priority was the game and the win.

Despite his successes, the coach didn't play him regularly. Alan was frustrated. At one game he became injured. He enjoyed a limousine ride as the team sent him home after the injury. He recalls that the team was to fly to and play in the Canary Islands the next day and he was being driven home as fireworks shot around him in celebration of the English holiday, "Guy Fawkes Day." You can sense the separation he felt as he spoke of this; separated from the team and separated from the common people.

He had his leg in a splint for several weeks. The team was down and doing poorly over those weeks. The coach told him he wanted him to play the next day. The trainer removed his splint and started bending Alan's knee. With youth on his side, he played that game and scored. His abilities had not been hampered. He came through when he was asked; yet he felt undervalued as he continued to play only intermittently.

He spoke angrily against a coach's decision that played a different player and resulted in a game loss. Alan told the coach directly that if he had been played they would have won. His boldness in his own abilities exceeded his shyness and the seriousness of competition coursed through him to the point of argument and occasionally player aggression. Losses were serious. It was a fight to victory in all manners. It was part of his drive.

Not long after, a scout noticed Alan. He was representing a new team and league in America. Alan was ripe for the opportunity to play as a regular and a star. He climbed on board, not knowing anything about the state of Minnesota, with the exception that there were teepees and log cabins. This was what he expected to see as he looked out his airplane window on his descent. Instead, he saw the modern state with looping freeways, skyscrapers, and a city swirling below.

His success skyrocketed. His fame took front pages in sports sections and magazines. He played exhibition games for the top-seated team in New York and played alongside Pele. This was following his game against that same team where he scored five goals. He traveled the world and played in front of huge crowds. Munich, Germany in front of 130,000 was a highlight, as well as Australia, New Zealand, Asia, Europe, Canada, and all over the U.S.A. In those travels he said he never had a camera. It was never about the travel, it was about the games and the stadiums.

This was thrilling to me. A world and life I could hardly imagine. I saw his work ethic and a man who gave his best. Now he wanted to give his best to me.

He was kind and seemed up for anything I thought to do. The only dark times were following losses or games poorly played. He closed up and became rigid until he had a chance to go at it again in practice or a game. I learned to stay quiet and not press him in those times.

Nearing Christmas, he helped me build a stable scene for my parents as a Christmas gift to them for their Nativity set. It was small and we knelt alongside each other holding the wood and hammering. I loved that moment and that project. In my heart I was trying to draw him into that very place, the place of his Savior's birth. He attended the Christmas Eve service with me at my home church and I felt so complete. My new engagement ring was on my finger. My heart was full and the part that continued to pull at me was the Lord. I tried to pull Alan in with me in small gestures that not even I recognized at the time.

Chapter 4

I Do

The summer came. The day we planned to be married was nearing. We went to England so that I could meet his family. The love, acceptance, and playfulness they poured out to me were overwhelming! His youngest sister was getting married and all of the excitement circling around that was immense.

I was thrust into the traditions of England in all manner of activity and food. What was lacking was my ability to understand their thick Geordie accent from the northeast. I spent days nodding and smiling until I finally broke down and cried. I bawled to Alan that I could not understand them. He must have said something to them to slow down or speak with less slang or else the cider I was drinking relieved my tension, because I started understanding them. It was wonderful!

On the night of his sister's wedding and reception, his mom burst into the bedroom where I was resting and blurted, "Your Mom is drunk!" She then closed the door as fast as she opened it and left. I know my eyes got wide as I giggled and felt completely part of his family. She called herself my mom. I was delighted!

She was a hard worker herself. She was typically quiet and busy. She put her all into her family. She had heartaches and never complained. To have had that moment of her complete joy and abandon, calling herself my mom for the first time, is a treasure even with the tipsy condition.

Alan and I talked about marrying in England. His sister was married in June by a justice of the peace, in a building which was quite beautiful and outside it had lovely gardens that cannot compare to any garden in the U.S. They had a reception in an upper level of an old stone building with family coming to his parents' house for the after party. It seemed quite wonderful to me, although my heart longed to be married in a church.

As it turned out, because of timing with the soccer season starting again and legal paperwork, we were married in the States. He was newly divorced and had already had the big wedding with his first marriage. I had no plans for anything big. I just wanted to be married to a man I loved and loved me. There was the hint of shame I carried, too. He had been married. His wife and two young children had moved back to England. I didn't want a public thing, and since his parents and family wouldn't be able to come for our wedding because finances wouldn't allow it, I kept the wedding small.

There was a lovely church made of honed stone built on the corner of a busy city block in downtown Minneapolis. It had a chapel that could be rented. Alan agreed to marry me there. I did not know the pastor. I was not a Presbyterian, as that was the denomination of the church. But it was Christian. It was beautiful with high ceilings, wooden pews; stained glass arching skyward and incredible ornate carvings framing the windows. It was as lovely as I hoped to find by comparison to the beautiful old buildings and churches in England. The pastor met with us before the wedding as was the requirement before he would marry people. I don't remember the conversation, other than some specifics about the ceremony.

The morning of the wedding, Alan dropped me off outside the church in my wedding dress as he drove to park the car in a nearby parking ramp. I stood outside waiting, alone and wondering if he was going to come back. I was shaking and believed he may have left me as my eyes searched up and down the streets for him. To my relief he came striding down the sidewalk toward me. I told him of my panic and he said, "Why would you ever think that?" We went inside and waited for the guests and wedding party. There were three, my parents and my brother. Mom handed me a lovely rose bouquet and had a boutonnière for Alan.

The pastor led the ceremony. We said our, "I do's," exchanged rings, and kissed. My parents signed our wedding license as the witnesses; my brother decorated the car with "Just Married" signs, streamers, and cans. They threw confetti and cheered. The peace, the settling, the giant sigh that followed as I finally exhaled after all that I had longed for had finally happened. I was married.

The soccer season started. So did the traveling. We missed each other terribly and he called often. I was one of the wives. The wives and serious girlfriends or fiancées gravitated to each other and spent those nights together when the men traveled. There is a closeness and sense of family that starts to happen. I would guess it is much like military families, only even much greater for them as those who serve the country are gone for much longer periods of time. The young adulthood in most of these professions brings about the newlyweds and new babies. It is a delightful time in life to share in these things with one another. There were babies born while their daddy's were gone and the women stood by one another counting contractions before sending the soon-to-be-mom off to the hospital. Times like that bond you. The memory lasts forever.

As life happened around us, Alan and I soon discussed the desire of having our own child together. After only 6 months of marriage, I had become pregnant. We were overjoyed!

In a rush coming out of nowhere I was filled with a heart change. I wanted to be the godly woman my parents raised. I wanted to raise this new child in prayer and salvation. The drinking stopped with that pregnancy and the sobriety of this new life growing in me grabbed me by both arms as I faced the reality of now becoming a mother. All that I had been raised with was flooding back, but my husband knew nothing of the depth of my faith. I had buried it for years. I ignored it to get what I wanted. I wanted to find love in a modern world my way. I begged Jesus for forgiveness for the way I lived. I needed Him. I wanted Him. I wanted my child to know Him too.

At a young age I had given my heart to Jesus. I had extended family who had attended a charismatic church in Iowa. We would attend services with them when we were in town for holidays. I grew up seeing healings, hearing prophecies, and watching the amazing work of the Holy Spirit. At a time of prayer when I was 12, the Lord gave me a filling of His Spirit and a prayer language of tongues—it is praying in a language that you do not know, but comes from within, from the place of His Spirit. The Spirit will pray when you don't know how to. I kept it quiet, with the exception of telling a few. My mom and I shared a lot with each other as she grew in her example of a woman who served the Lord with her whole heart.

Many of my prayers were answered as a child. The Lord showed His faithfulness, love, and mercies. He changed classroom settings for me. He healed my broken hip at the age of 16 when He pieced the bone back just before surgery as the latest X-ray proved. He showed me His grandeur and presence on a mountaintop experience in Mexico on a mission trip with my youth group. He was powerfully there anytime I looked to Him.

Why I had buried that so deep is a mystery. I remained blind to the fullness of the Lord. I clung to the idea that the man I married was the fulfillment of me, my life, and future. Happily ever after was the fairytale hope on earth.

Now I was married, we were having a child, and I was living my faith alone. I prayed for baby daughter as she grew in me. I would look into the sky at the stars and think about the man she would marry someday. I prayed for him and his family.

What remained in common was that Alan and I shared our sense for fun and laughter together. That has been a magnet that carries a large attraction we have for one another. We love to make one another laugh and laughter "does good like a medicine." It helped cover some of the painful sores that come when the yoke is not equal.

He did not grow up saying "I'm sorry." He did not understand forgiveness. He could stay mad and not talk for days. He was used to arguing in his first marriage. It was a habit and one that was hard to break. He wouldn't accept responsibility in our disagreements, but would ignore it or blame me. Of course, there were things I was responsible for too. I held a lot in and my actions would come out by being cold or sarcastic.

He suffered. He had been in a failing marriage and I was an easy and ready lure to move onto. He missed his children from his first marriage terribly. He would grieve even more on their birthdays, and the grief would turn to frustration and more anger. They were in England and the volatility of his relationship with his first wife made it nearly impossible for him to communicate with his children. He was suffering a great loss. I had such hopes that our child would help soothe some of that pain for him.

I prayed for him, I prayed for them, and I prayed for us.

Soccer helped him take out frustrations. He could run until he dropped, he could kick and scream. The outdoor game had changed to an indoor style in an attempt to keep American fans engaged as the league made major changes with teams folding and new ones starting. It was played on hockey rinks and incorporated the use of the boards into the game. Alan loved watching hockey and he seemed to adjust fine to this new way of play. The length of the field was shorter; the goals smaller, a thin layer of green Astroturf was placed on top of the ice to run on and yet, Alan continued to succeed.

Our daughter, Kendra, was born and Alan was at my side. We held our precious bundle and saw the miracle of God's creation so complete in nine short months. I was in awe of what He made and how much I loved her. Alan was all over her too. An experienced daddy, he showed me how to change the diapers and he helped me dress her. Shortly after we returned from the hospital, the Minneapolis paper sent a photographer and writer to our house for pictures of our new family to put in a large section of their sports page. The limelight even fell on an infant.

I was one of the lucky wives. I was from the town of the team for whom my husband played. Most players were not American and many had wives from the country that they were from or if she was American, from the town they met in when they played for a different team. I felt the blessing of having my child, my parents, and friends seated all around me at Alan's games. I also sensed the longing of the other women for their families far away. It is what drives the wives even closer to one another as we become one another's family. My parents loved those ladies and their babies too. The wives came to games all dressed up with our babies dolled up, too. We'd pass the babies up and down the row of seats to coo over them while mixing it up for a shout on a play or stand and cheer for a goal in our high heels.

One of my mom's favorite memories from those days was when Alan was fully dressed in uniform wearing his cleats, shin guards, socks, shorts, and jersey before a big game. He was bent over a stroller filled with our plump, baby girl in pink and lace as he changed her diaper. Then, he was off to the locker room for the final pep talk before the game started.

If the team lost the game, Alan would be angry. He'd be mad at others' mistakes or coaching that he disagreed with or frustrated with himself. He would often be quiet and not want to talk or sometimes collect me and head straight home instead of staying back and socializing with the other players and their wives in the Observatory Club.

After one loss, I wanted to stay. The Turtles, a band from the past, was performing after the game. The team's organization often hosted additional entertainment as a draw for the games. He didn't want to listen to the concert so he stayed in the Observatory Club. The club was for members, players, or those with passes so it was relatively private. I took our baby daughter into the stands, to an empty row up high in the back of the stadium, and I listened. I waited to hear them sing one of my favorite songs, "So Happy Together." I enjoyed it as much as I could, despite the empty pain and the irony of the words as I thought of Alan and me. Much of our time really was apart and not always so happy.

Life for him was a world I couldn't completely understand. I saw that gifted athletes are wired differently. There is an intensity in most all that they do and when interested, the emotions are equally intense. There is a noticeable separation between those of this caliber and those who are not. There is also an incredible camaraderie in those who share the same gifting. It is in part why he enjoyed being with his teammates so much.

The loneliness that my life had become as I rode a roller coaster of emotions with a husband whose every fiber of his being was about the win was part of the package in marrying a professional athlete like him. It is part of what made him as good as he was. My only way of helping that seemed tolerable to him after a loss or a poor game was to tell him I loved him, kneel down next to him, and kiss him on his forehead as he would lie on the couch with eyes closed tightly and brow furrowed. I would get up and leave him be as I prayed and asked the Lord to help him through it.

At games I often noticed the other wives looking sensitively to their husbands too, and read the upset following a poor personal performance or game. They too, would whisk themselves quietly home. None of us ever talked about it. It was an unspoken knowing. It also left us as wives, uncomforted, by keeping it private and doing it alone.

Still, there were great joys in this life. His off-season gave us months together where we could travel to England to see his family for extended stays. During the season, he was home from practice by lunch time. His trips for out-of-town games were always shorter than a week long, so we had a lot of time together, too. It was fun and there was no one else with whom I'd rather have been.

Chapter 5

Money

About the money...he was one of the top-paid players on the team, which afforded us the ability to buy nice gifts for family, have nice furniture, and cars. I didn't have to work and could be with our daughter. But, as a soccer player in the United States, the pay scale was significantly lower than other professional athletes.

Locally, our city had a television show that was much like a variety show with home improvement tips, shopping, and human interest stories. I was asked to be on it with our daughter and model some fashions for a segment with other local professional athletes' wives and children from football, baseball, and hockey. I was the famous soccer player's wife.

As we gathered ahead of time to get the clothing from the high-end store that was featuring the fashion trends, the women made incredible purchases as they wanted to own what they were wearing or what their child was wearing. I staggered at the price tags as they nonchalantly pulled out their money and purchased additional items along with the items they were going to be wearing.

We did our segment days later. I had never experienced a green room before or had been on that end of the camera. I was startled at the crudeness of the studio—the "Green Room" was painted cement blocks and inside there were old stained couches and chairs. As our clothing was brought into us with our names on the garment bags, we began to open them up and get dressed.

The women had stayed to themselves and their children. There wasn't any visiting or interacting. One of the baseball player's wives pulled out her dress. It was two sizes smaller than what she was to wear. In a panic, she tried to put it on as she exclaimed, "It's the wrong size!" The women all stopped what we were doing and helped pull the fabric together, squeeze, and finally zip her in. We had a lot more in common with each other than the concerns of wardrobe malfunctions. But, it lives to be a secret lived alone.

The show started. Our little one-year-old daughter, Kendra, was precious and drew the biggest "awwws" from the studio audience as I set her down in her darling white stockings, black shiny shoes with a strap, and the puffy red-and-black-checked dress with a velvet bow. She was the youngest child featured of the famous dads.

Things seemed to be going well. His team won division finals, then made it to the final round against the five-time champions, the San Diego Sockers. Alan's team, the Strikers, came in second. It was a placement that has forever given us sympathy and compassion for the guys who have played their hearts out in any sport that made it into the finals just to come up short in one crucial game. It is heart wrenching. Alan still won MVP, but it paled to the championship loss.

Not long after, the owners of the Strikers decided to fold the team. I wasn't worried. I didn't know any better. I assumed he was this great star. He would have a team soon. Alan, on the other hand, carried great concern and the weight of worry over the unknown. He was aware of the intricacies of teams folding, leagues shutting down, a pool of players without teams to compete, and he was getting older. Age is the most common end to a player's career. I was also pregnant with our second child.

We would learn of different players signing on with other teams. One of them got the dream signing of playing for the unsurpassed San Diego Sockers. Not long after, Alan was called by San Diego and asked to play, too. His contract offer was half of what he was making in Minnesota. He said yes, and we packed up for southern California. I was thrilled and had always wanted to live there. It was an easy move for me.

The team paid for the moving expenses. We went down to one car because of the money decrease that came in his contract and we looked for a place to rent. Then the reality of the experience started to hit. I was away from my family and friends for the first time. I became friends with a few of the wives in San Diego, but it was breaking in with a group that was pretty well established. Some super fans befriended us and became parent-like to us. But yet, the loneliness was immense. Alan was gone more often. The away games were more days away because of the distance flying from San Diego verses central Minnesota. He played less because they already had their own established stars. He was frustrated and I moped.

As we drifted further apart, I felt spiritually starved. We didn't have a church there, and I didn't have my mom's ear to pray with or share with. Amidst the beauty of all that God made in such an incredible creation of southern California, I didn't notice Him. I longed for more of Him but I didn't even notice Him standing right there with me on that beach in the faithfulness of one wave coming to the shore after another, from that endless Pacific Ocean.

Our second daughter, Kristin, was born. I had prayed over her, too, while she was growing in me. I prayed for her future husband and family as well. I lifted Alan before the Lord and asked God to care for him and help him to find joy with me again. He was present for Kristin's birth, but had to leave for a road trip shortly after. My father had come out to San Diego with my mom for her birth and my dad was the one who brought my daughter and me home from the hospital. It was a strange feeling, but part of this life.

Most of Alan's joy was found on the golf course with team mates. He loved me. But, my ideas weren't at all matching his. I would want to go to the beach with him and the kids. That was the last place he wanted to go because he had run miles on it in training that morning. When he would return from road trips I would want to go out to dinner. He would rather have a home-cooked meal because he'd spent the week eating out. I hadn't thought those things out. I didn't have the sense or sensitivity. Instead, I focused on myself and let myself feel hurt.

Not having a church, not having close friends or family or a husband who knew anything about my beliefs, I baptized our newest darling daughter in our bathtub while he was on a road trip. I prayed in the Spirit over her, crying for her life to be filled and lived fully for Him. Kendra, then two years old, was taking a nap and got up and joined in the "service." She had been baptized in my home church with friends and family around. Alan understood the ceremony of tradition and had been present for hers, but did not understand the full meaning of it.

I grew up with infant baptisms and I also was baptized by submersion by my dad in our backyard pool when I was an older child. I remembered how significant it was when he did that for our family and I felt like I was, as a parent, to go ahead and baptize Kristin, even as a baby. I held her gently in my arms, keeping her head up above the water in the bath tub and drizzled water with my other hand on her downy head.

Some of our best times while living in California were team picnics that we went to every Sunday that the team was in town. It was planned privately amongst ourselves. That was our family gathering time and day of rest. Those picnics were wonderful and we never had to check the weather. It was always sunny and 72 degrees. We met at Mission Park while the kids ran and chased. Babies napped in strollers, kites were flown and parents flopped down on the green grass next to each other. It was always friendly and fun. There's something about being out in the sunshine with children that brings a sense of purity.

As the season continued, the team did well. Once again, they were playing in the final championship series. As the team's streak continued, The San Diego Sockers won the championship again. Alan had played for a championship team. He received a championship ring, doused teammates in champagne and experienced all of the joy that comes with winning! A victory celebration was planned at the stadium and each player and his wife and children were driven out into the center of the field in a limousine. I rubbed the leather interior and peeked in to the compartments and looked through the dark glass. It was a brief drive from the loading area to the center of the field. We opened the door, stepped out onto the field and felt the bright lights that shone down from the stadium filled with cheering fans. It would be the last time he would be on a field as a professional player.

Alan spoke with the coach shortly after and told him we had planned to go to England in the off-season and spend some time in Minnesota. The coach told him to go ahead, enjoy the time off, and they would discuss a contract when he returned. He told Alan that he was definitely in their plans for next year. We put our things in storage, vacated our apartment, and left.

Returning from England and stopping in Minnesota, Alan placed a call to the coach to check in. He was told that they signed two younger guys instead. The season was to start in three short weeks. Teams were set. Alan was shocked!

Alan put a fast call in to his agent. The man scrambled to find a team that hadn't used their salary cap and had room on their team. He called Alan back some days later and said that Dallas would take him, but the pay would be half what he'd been making in San Diego. Once again, I prayed hard for help.

It was his choice. Alan decided it was time to end his soccer career. It was time to stay in Minnesota and start real life. He recently told me that after winning the championship game, while players were celebrating still, he sat down on the locker room bench and thought to himself, "I think I just played my last game as a professional player."

CHAPTER 6

For Richer or Poorer

Beginning something new, we had to look squarely into life's eyes. Our home in Minnesota had renters in it and we ended up needing to sell it. Our belongings that were in storage in San Diego were put in a moving van. It was a moving van that we had to pay for ourselves this time.

My brother moved out to San Diego shortly after we did. He continued living there and assisted the mover with emptying our storage unit along with my parents who were out there visiting him. Again, my brother was there to rescue me. Eventually, San Diego was where my brother met his wife.

Without a place to stay, my parents took us in. I began school to get a real estate license and so did Alan. We were real estate agents without a home.

Starting a new business is expensive and takes time. We were young in that field and old for sports. My parents blessed us by letting us stay with them. My mom was busy with her own job, running a house with six people in it along with helping watch our very young daughters when Alan and I were not in. Dad worked too. He did a lot of government work, and had many patents in fields often labeled "Top Secret." The stress from his work was not very easily relieved when he would return home to a loud, full house.

We quickly went through our savings and continued to struggle. Alan learned that real estate was not for him. He was always used to being the one approached, not the one having to do the approaching. But, God used it for Alan. Computer programs were coming fast into the business and Alan had a knack for understanding them. The real estate company we worked for had Alan teach other agents how to use the computer. He enjoyed that, but it didn't pay much and was not dependable.

A friend in the real estate company with us knew we were struggling. Her husband owned a small landscaping business and they needed help. Alan began working for her husband for a low hourly wage. Anything helped. Again, I saw Alan's incredible work ethic and efforts to support us.

I watched him, with my heart breaking, come home after 12- to 14-hour days in the summer heat covered in mud and sweat. Here was this incredible thoroughbred of a gifted athlete using his body as a plow horse. He dug post holes, laid boulders, set retaining walls, and hauled trees with root balls wrapped in burlap. He did it all with humility and with appreciation for the work. The truck used by the men who would pick him up and drop him off was dented, rusted, and filled with rocks and dirt. It was a far cry from the limousine in which he had once been seated. As my heart ached for him, I fell even more in love with him.

His greatest frustration was being under the head of another man's house. It was hard to let go of that position of authority, and instinctually there were times of argument in an effort to determine dominance. Being the daughter and the wife, it left me hurting for both my father and my husband as they were forced to collide in an unnatural situation at this time in our lives. Dad knew he needed to help and Alan knew we needed the help.

Following one of those encounters and in Alan's exhaustion he cried to me in the basement of the house. It was more than he could take. I begged him to ask Jesus into his heart. "Jesus can calm and give peace and take the hurts and burdens from you. He loves you so much, Alan." He just rolled over on the bed holding his hands tight to his forehead with his eyes squeezed shut. I rubbed his back and then stepped away. The next day he told me he got on his knees and asked Jesus into his heart. He said he felt tingles inside. Later, he would have no memory of this.

As my longing for more of the Lord continued I joined a mom's Bible study group at church. We met in the afternoon and brought along our children so that they could play together. They were kind, godly women and had families that centered their lives on Christ. I felt alone.

My husband wasn't like theirs. I felt like I didn't measure up and eventually I stopped coming to the study. I made the assumption that they wouldn't understand. I also made the assumption that they would judge me and think we were terrible. It is amazing what selfish condemnation can do. As I look back at these women, not a one of them would have condemned me, but would have had compassion and prayed for us. I walked away from the strength that could have been and from the prayers that could have lifted me.

One of the women knew of our financial struggle and that we were living with my parents. When Thanksgiving time came she put our names on the church list to have food sent to help with Thanksgiving. A car pulled up to our house and people began unloading bag after bag after bag of food. They poured out blessings. My mom was getting bags thrust into her arms as she said, "You don't need to do this—we are able to help them!"

The bags wouldn't stop. It was humbling for her and for all of us. The food blessed us and blessed my parents as they had a time of relief. No one would have believed what life had turned into for us. None of us saw it coming. This was probably the day that revealed how low we were. It also was a day that showed us the Lord was there. He brought the food to our door through His precious children, the Church.

We lived with my parents for three years. During that time Alan left real estate and started schooling for computer programming and networking. When he finished he began looking for a job. This brought another unexpected result.

Knowing his name recognition in Minnesota, we thought surely this would help open doors. We were wrong. Doors shut. As he would go through the interview process the interviewers assumed, and even stated in the interview, "We are sorry, we won't be able to pay you what you are used to, or position you high." Alan didn't care about that. He needed to start somewhere, he needed a beginning. Rejection after rejection came on the heels of name recognition. If only they could have seen how hard he worked, even in the mud and mire of landscaping. He's smart and he catches on quickly. None of that rose above their assumptions of a famous athlete.

After begging God for months for a job for Alan, one came. He started literally staffing people for mail rooms; the iconic first step of beginnings—the mail room. I praised the Lord and thanked him for giving this to Alan. Alan had purpose again, a new satisfaction and something for which to strive. He is a hard worker and anyone that would hire him had made a good investment. Alan needed to know computer software programs and helped lay things out as the temporary staffing agency was on the road to growth.

With Alan's job came our ability to purchase our own home. A charming 700-square-foot home with two bedrooms and no basement was for sale. It had a fenced yard for the children and the backyard was huge. It was perfect! It was near my parents, so the girls, who had become so close to their grandparents after spending such tender years of their lives living in their house, were able to visit them easily. Thank you, Jesus!

Financially we still struggled. I baked my own bread to save money and used dishtowels instead of plastic wrap or baggies and more. We had relatives pass down clothes to our girls as they grew into their cousins' things. We rarely ate out. The girls did not grow up knowing what McDonald's was like for a long time. I remember being so grateful to a neighbor who took the girls for an ice cream cone one time at Dairy Queen. It was a treat we couldn't afford. I never thought to seek government aid. I hadn't grown up knowing about it so we survived on our own.

A cousin of mine had just been married and he and his new bride stopped by following their honeymoon. We celebrated with a bottle of champagne that had been given to us at New Year's along with some affordable popsicles that we had. The differences that life can bring stood strong in the mixing of those two things—champagne and popsicles. We enjoyed it, celebrating their new union and lives together. They were a couple embarking on life's journey completely solid and united in their faith. While dating, they even waited for their first kiss until it was their wedding day.

He was attending seminary school and had graduated from Northwestern in St. Paul. She had been a personal secretary to Edith Schaeffer, author and wife of famed theologian Francis Schaeffer. My cousin, in honoring his promise as an enrolled student, did not drink the champagne. He did, however, jump at the suggestion that I made that he taste it from the kiss of his new bride's lips.

I sat impressed at his ability to withhold from drinking and the seriousness that he took in his vows to the school and certainly in his new marriage. Champagne and popsicles were made precious to me as the fairytale of a marriage sound in shared faith started tugging at my heart.

Chapter 7

Differences

Things were getting more solid financially. Alan was getting raises, and I was doing better with real estate. This afforded him the ability to golf again.

He had met some friends through his computer school. He hadn't had male friendships since his soccer days. It was hard to keep those old friendships in the midst of the humility of what life had become. Again, it was a seclusion of shame.

His new friends hadn't been soccer fans and really didn't know that part of him, other than the knowledge that he had once been a professional athlete. The hard part for me was that they were all single. When they would golf, I would be home all day without another woman who was going through the same thing.

He also started working longer hours, not coming home for lunch like he used to, and shutting down more at home. As our companionship was becoming out of reach, I reached for Jesus even more.

I dove into gardening for a hobby. Our huge yard made it easy to grow all kinds of vegetables, raspberries, and my newfound love, roses. I joined a rose club that met once a month on Friday nights. It had become my new date night with other rosarians and an opportunity to get excited about all of the varieties of roses. I find my attraction to roses to be much of the way I look at people. I see the beauty and ignore the thorns. I dove into this hobby so fully that

I began showing roses in the British and American style competitions once a year, finding recognition through ribbons and awards.

I didn't go out with girlfriends anymore. Alan was always jealous or suspected that women only met to talk about and look for men. I didn't understand why he thought like that. If I did go out with my girlfriends, it wasn't worth what I had to come home to. He wouldn't talk to me and I would feel guilty that I had gone.

Things were becoming more volatile as I closed up from other women to try to keep the peace. My happy place was the garden. It was at this time that I learned to really walk with the Lord day by day. I praised Him and thanked Him for the beautiful creation I was able to enjoy. I would lie on my stomach in the green grass and reach my arms out hugging it as if I was hugging the Lord.

I cried to Him and laughed to Him and praised Him as He showed more of Himself in the beautiful outdoor world I was living. I prayed hard for our daughters and over them for their lives, friendships, schooling, and growing up. It wasn't an easy home in which to grow up.

Many times Alan would become so agitated that he would pack a suitcase and threaten to leave. He did it at night after the girls had gone to bed. He'd fill it with underwear and other essentials. I would cry and beg him to stay. He'd set the case down and stay or he would leave for an hour or two and come back. This happened countless times and was almost a routine. So many times I would tell him that Jesus loved him and could help him. I would remind him of the miracle he had of his own health restored at a young age after meningitis and that God had loved him so much to have healed him and then gifted him with incredible athletic abilities.

His frequent response was, "I'll NEVER be like you! I will never talk about God like you do!" It hurt, but somehow I managed to not give up and continued to pray for him to know a life with Jesus.

I continued to make sure our girls went to Sunday school. I knew Alan was not comfortable with me being around other women. I too, was uncomfortable being around other church women because I felt ashamed. So, to serve the Lord, I taught Sunday school to preschoolers. I could dive in there, loving them as I do, without the threat to my husband and marriage.

Attending church alone or with the girls for so many years had some people assuming I was a single parent. Alan would make appearances for Christmas and Easter or when the girls had their yearly spring musical. I loved those days as he sat next to me. I would hold his hand and wait to hear if he would raise his voice in a song or I would strain, in sideway glances, to see if the message was reaching him; always looking for a sign of hope.

Peace would still find a way of reaching me in the midst of the turmoil of my life as I leaned and learned from Jesus. But as I did grow closer toward the ways of the Lord, I got carried away in what I thought was the "look" of a saintly woman.

As I had become engrossed in growing our own vegetables and baking as I did, I began to live a "Little House on the Prairie" life. I'd go so far to say that my underpants probably resembled Laura Ingall's, too. You can imagine.

I allowed myself to get distanced from being a wife and the sexy woman that first attracted my husband as he distanced himself from me. At the time I felt "good." I was a "good" woman. There is a need, I have learned, that women need to understand as they walk with Christ, that He also created marriage and all of the sexual joy that comes with it. I didn't get that and our marriage suffered. If you find yourself convicted of that, I would recommend the book *Sheet Music*. It is a wonderful Christian book on the sexual part of marriage and it can be very freeing in a glorious way to see God in all parts of your life, even the bedroom!

Adding more difficulty to our marriage, Alan's mom died from cancer at age 57. That year rocked Alan. Everything seemed to be coming down on him. His anger was increasing, and if he wasn't yelling he wasn't talking. He was losing weight. He was miserable in our house. Winter was hard because he didn't have a physical outlet like golf. He became restless, then lethargic.

By chance—or as I now see, God's prompting—I was given a brochure on depression. Alan had said that he wished he could drive himself off of a bridge and that we would all be happier. He sobbed and I shared that I just read about depression and it sounded like he may have it. I read the symptoms to him from the brochure. I told him that he might be able to get help. I was shaking and terrified for him as I watched him crumbling in front of me.

I made an appointment with the only person he would be comfortable. It was his team doctor from when he played professionally. This physician treated athletes for multiple professional teams besides soccer. Alan didn't want to go in alone. He insisted I go in with him. As we waited for the doctor to come into the room, the time was dragging. Alan became agitated and frantic, he wanted to leave. Just as he almost walked out, the doctor came in.

Upon checking Alan and talking with him, the doctor quickly diagnosed him with depression. Depression in the 1990s was not as commonly heard about or diagnosed. The doctor made two comments to me. One was, "Why did you wait so long to bring him in?!" The other was, "The bigger they are, the harder they fall."

I was furious! I was relieved for the diagnosis, but how was I to know what it was? The other upset was that the doctor knew how hard it is for athletes after they finish playing. He must have seen it over and over as they once had been so big in the eyes of the public, only to fall into the pit of loss. I was grateful that he was someone that Alan trusted, but as one of the wives, I was shattered that no one had ever warned us.

All of the marriages that I saw end in divorce amongst the athletes after they finished playing probably suffered similar things. No one talks about it! No one warns you! No one prepares you! Only by the grace of God did He put in me the tenacity to honor my wedding vows. For richer for poorer, for better or worse, in sickness and in health, I hung on.

At one time he had the fame, the adoration, the success in God-given skills and all of the satisfaction that came with it. Then it was gone overnight. His searching in other ways was not fulfilling. When it couldn't be reached, he crashed.

Anti-depression medication made a big difference for Alan in exactly the amount of time the doctor thought he may start to feel better. He was less gloomy, less agitated, and less hopeless. I thanked Jesus. I continued to hold onto the need to let other wives and players know that this condition happens sometimes for athletes. I never figured out a way or a platform, so I took to praying for them as I saw them on television.

I continued to pray hard for Alan, asking the Lord to help him completely overcome the depression. God once again blessed Alan. Eventually, he no longer needed the medication.

Chapter 8
Flourish

Real estate was improving even more for me. Alan was given many responsibilities with his company and he received more raises. We moved to a larger home that the Lord provided. I had prayed for a home on one side of a two-block stretch. It was a specific prayer. As Alan and I took a neighborhood walk we asked people we met along the way if they knew of anyone selling. Some people on the street told us of a family that was considering selling in the next year.

We continued our walk and went up to the home to inquire about it. They invited us right in. Just a few short months later, the house was ours. Prior to moving in, Alan and I had been for a walk admiring the home as we waited in contract for final loan approval. As I peeked at the window, I saw the owners standing with arms on each other's shoulders dancing and bopping their heads side to side. I giggled and told Alan about it. I hoped that the same joy would be there for us.

The woman of the home told me she had been praying for whoever God wanted to have this home, that the buyers would be good people for their neighbors. She and I had opportunities to share our faith with one another. Praise God, He chose us. We were coming into a home that had been filled with prayer.

The biggest financial obstacle coming would be a roof that soon needed replacing. As I prayed about it,

I heard a distinct voice of the Lord. He said, "Windfall." As I was learning to listen to the voice of the Lord, He often spoke to me in one or two words as He knew I wasn't a very good listener. His one or two words would remain memorable and with me. Within that first year a tremendous windstorm came to our area and the sky poured out hail stones the size of golf balls. We called our insurance adjuster out, just as everyone in the area was doing. We were given a whole new roof completely covered by our homeowner's insurance. This was another mighty way that the Lord showed me His hand. I praised and praised and thanked Him.

As things were better financially, we were able to enjoy other things. We were able to eat out again. I was buying plastic wrap and enjoying every roll of it. We got a boat and spent hours of family time boating. Alan still loved his golfing and I continued to garden and pray. The marriage difficulties were less, but not gone. The empty void was still there.

Our daughters were growing and becoming more independent in their teens. My womanly advice to them as they began dating was to never cry over the 't-shirt boy,' sharing the story of my first date and how I ended up with the one on the field. My other advice was not to pinch anyone's bum unless they really meant it.

I threw myself into my real estate work and again asked the Lord to make it His business and that He would use me. I asked Him to help me do well. I continued to pray for Alan, too.

Incredible blessings came at His hand. I ended up being the top real estate producer for my company and was given an award in front of hundreds of other agents. Following the ceremony, some other real estate agents came up to me and asked me how I did it. I told them I prayed. I said, "God was the real estate agent and I just drove the car." This was the first time I spoke out publicly like this to co-workers. I couldn't help myself, it just came flying out. Some of them got big smiles and others furrowed their brows and didn't understand. I believe the Lord gave me that year in order to speak of His glory.

Shortly after, Alan was contacted by the National Soccer Hall of Fame out of New York. He was told that he was being inducted into the Soccer Hall of Fame. He was being honored for his outdoor soccer performances. He was the second highest all-time goal scorer for that league.

This was an incredible honor and blessing. Our girls, who did not remember seeing their dad in association with soccer, were going to be able to witness it themselves.

The four of us flew out to New York where once again Alan was treated like royalty. We toured through the facility, were given countless souvenirs, hotel accommodations, and the best of cuisine for the weekend. There was an entire display—a life-sized banner of Alan and photos from Alan's soccer career. Our daughters were amazed, as were Alan and I.

The blessings didn't stop there. Alan was to be honored with a teammate of his, Ace (Patrick) Ntsoelengoe. Ace was being inducted at the same time as Alan. Ace flew in with his family from South Africa for the induction. It was a joyous reunion for these teammates—years back, Ace played alongside Alan, making the passes as a midfielder for Alan to score. You couldn't find a kinder, gentler, softer-spoken man than Ace. His skill spoke loudly for him instead. His mannerisms and gentility were mesmerizing.

Even our daughters were taken by Ace, his family, and the love and joy they had with each other.

Alan was also blessed by the attendance of his former teammate and coach for the indoor league with the Minnesota Strikers, Alan Merrick. The generosity that Alan Merrick and his wife Mary exhibited in being there in New York for Alan and Ace will never be forgotten.

Alan had to make an acceptance speech at the induction ceremony banquet. He spoke clearly and well. He had humor and knowledge, and people hung to his words. Our girls and I sat in amazement as we listened. We knew Alan's shyness and his nervousness and watched all of that seemingly melt away before our eyes. He was able to publicly acknowledge before all of the people that the level of his success was greatly attributed to his quiet and humble teammate, Ace, during those years that he played for the Minnesota Kicks.

Following the last scheduled event of the weekend, we had several hours before our plane was to leave in the evening. We made a trip into the Adirondack Mountains in our rental car. It was fall in upstate New York. The colors of the turning and falling leaves against a gray sky, the gentle rain and dark rained-soaked ground were vibrant. With every turn, the next scene was just as beautifully painted.

Our daughter had recently acquired a CD of praise and worship music performed by a couple from our church. Alan was quiet as the weekend's events were soaking in and he drove through the mountains. Amazingly, he didn't complain about the music and he didn't pop the CD out. The music filled me and filled our car as I praised the Lord quietly inside for all He had given and all He had created.

The Hall of Fame induction seemed to erase the pain of the ending of his career. He was given fresh acknowledgment and appreciation for all he did for the sport. He felt better and so did I. Our girls now had an understanding of the greatness of what their father had once been.

The local papers caught up with the honor and wrote an article about Alan. Alan Merrick organized some events for some of the teammates to reunite again. It felt good for Alan to see more of his past teammates. Alan was also invited to play in some celebrity golf tournaments. A television station did a sports spot, bringing in Alan and a few of the players who had remained in Minneapolis together for an interview and a look back on their playing careers. It was more healing for him.

Three years later, Alan was contacted by the president of the Hall of Fame and told Alan that Ace was found dead in his car from a massive heart attack just south of Johannesburg, South Africa. The opportunity that Alan had in New York to reunite across the globe with Ace, to thank him and acknowledge him, had really been a gift. Both Alan and Ace were born in 1956.

The summer before our oldest daughter, Kendra, was to begin her senior year in high school and our youngest, Kristin, was about to begin her sophomore year brought more considerations. I was looking into a future that would be very different for me. As Alan had busied himself with work and other interests, I was seeing that much of my time would be empty since our daughters would soon be leaving home.

In a heartfelt prayer on my knees in our family room, I earnestly asked the Lord for blessings for Alan and me. I asked Him to give us a bond, to keep us active in the community, to draw us closer together and give us a common interest that we both would love. I asked this prayer through tears of otherwise anticipated emptiness.

Three months later, Alan found me asleep on the family room couch in the middle of the afternoon. I never napped. As he stood surprised to find me, I awakened. He asked if I felt okay and I told him that I did, I was just really tired. Then he asked me if I was pregnant.

This question jolted me. I thought I had been going through the beginnings of menopause. I went to the drug store and found test kits side by side for menopause and pregnancy. I didn't know which to grab. I thought I'd rule out the pregnancy right away. I asked the pharmacist if I took the pregnancy test and I was going through menopause, would I get a false positive? He said no, so, I bought the pregnancy test.

The kit said that it needed to sit for one minute before seeing the results. They were wrong. There was the positive mark. It showed up in seconds. I couldn't believe it! I started giggling. I told Alan and he started laughing, too. We both laughed together in shock and amazement that we were going to be parents again at this time in life. Our reaction was definitely us. We enjoyed a good joke and felt like one had been played on us.

As it all began to sink in I remembered...the prayer! There it was! All answered in one little bundle; a bond, active in the community, drawn closer together, a common interest we both loved. Here I had been imagining that the Lord was going to have me take up golf!

I rushed out to the library looking for any type of self-help book. Surely there was something titled

"Old Mom." Nope, no such luck. We were going to be winging this one.

As Alan became more serious over the new baby coming, he said, "It's like a second chance." He was feeling like this time he was ready to really participate in the raising of a child.

Over the last few years Alan had come to church more often. He sat with me because he knew it pleased me. He was even willing to put his hands on my stomach along with me as I prayed out loud for this new little baby. It was the first time we ever did that together.

At Alan's suggestion, he asked if I liked the name Samuel. I loved it! Little did he know that in my sixteen years of teaching Sunday school to preschoolers, my favorite Bible lesson to teach was about Samuel. He was a child who heard and listened to God. He grew up serving the Lord. We had a harder time selecting a girl's name. Of course, as God would have it, our baby was a boy. Samuel.

Chapter 9

Rocked

Samuel was born nine weeks early, despite efforts to keep me from delivering during a weeklong stay in the hospital. I was given injections to help lung development for the possibility of a premature birth. Prayers filled my hospital room. Friends, our pastor, and family from afar and I prayed continuously for this little baby. Two days after the injections, he was born.

A team of doctors and nurses from the children's hospital as well as the delivery team were there as Samuel was being born. They waited expectantly for this emergency situation, prepared to run him to oxygen and breathing equipment and anything else an infant would need being born so early. Alan was at my side.

As he was born, Alan said he came out spiraling like a football as the doctor scrambled to make the catch. The crew of doctors and nurses cheered and exclaimed, "He's breathing!!!" This little three-pound baby was able to be wrapped, carried to us, and held by the doctor long enough for Alan and me to see him before they whisked him away. As he was held over my chest, I instantly prayed out loud that God would make us worthy parents of Samuel and praised God for the strength he had to breathe. Alan bowed his head too. Then, quietly and under my breath, I prayed in the Spirit. I couldn't help it. Alan leaned in and whispered, asking what I was doing. It stopped and I didn't answer.

We went through the crazy world of parenting kids in high school and having the wide gap of having a baby with no other children in between to transition. It was proms, competitions, driver's licenses, boyfriends, college, and diapers. Our little guy was growing up in a house full of teenagers and their friends. He learned to keep their hours, staying up late and sleeping in.

It was more fun than we'd ever expect. It was also a lot harder physically as my forty-something and his fifty-something year-old arms ached with carrying a little one again. We took turns rubbing on the muscle ointment and smelled like old people until Samuel was able to walk. Months after he was born, our oldest daughter, Kendra, let us in on a secret. She said that she had prayed for a baby brother every day when she was ten years old. She wasn't too thrilled with God's timing, but she was thrilled with her baby brother.

Alan was all over this little guy. He attended all of the scheduled doctor's visits and immunizations with me. He dressed him, diapered him, and gave him his bottles and food. He even brought him to work to show him off there.

Participation had been growing with Alan in the last couple of years. He attended more of our daughters' events. He was going to church more often with me, too. It was all things that I had hoped for and prayed for. I soaked up every minute of it.

When the familiar distancing started to return, I noticed it more sharply. I wanted our closeness back. I wanted his love and attention like it had just been. I started to feel invisible. When Samuel needed a doctor visit and another round of immunizations, Alan didn't go this time. It wasn't like him. The memories of parenting alone were coming back. So was his shortness with me. Our oldest daughter had been recently engaged and I was making wedding arrangements for her alone.

After a couple of months of this distancing, I made a discovery that no wife ever wants to make. Alan was having an affair. I didn't want to believe it. I did multiple things to prove to myself it was really happening. It was.

My entire body started to shake and quake. My world, not perfect, was not even close to what I had thought. It was a lie. On the afternoon of verifying the truth of the infidelity, Alan was golfing. When he returned from golf he told me that on one of the holes hail came pouring down on them and it was frightening. I stared knowingly at him. I didn't tell him of my discovery then. But the time of the hail was when I had received absolute proof. I didn't know where this was going, but I knew God was there in the raining down of the hail.

I waited two days before making the confrontation, timing it so they would be together. He was shaken, as I shook. He looked terrified and pale. He left her and ran to me.

I finally broke down. I cried, I ached, I shook and shuddered. I felt more pain than I ever thought was possible. My body was nauseated. My throat was tight as I could scarcely swallow food. What I did swallow would rarely stay in. The intensity of emotion was throwing my entire body out of control as I felt so out of control.

We went through this very privately. I did go to our pastor right away and sought prayer and help.

I told him I hurt for the young woman that he had been with, too. I wanted to give her a Bible to show her how God loved her and wanted her to live. After a while, that sense of compassion turned into anger as I held onto bitterness.

Alan strove to do things right. He came home on time. He texted me so I could know his every move. I continued to check on him secretly and publicly. I did not share with my family or friends about what had happened with the exception of my mom—I didn't want anyone to tell me what to do. I wanted to make my own choices and my mom left me to that.

I prayed hard. I told Alan he needed Jesus. I begged Jesus to give Alan a godly man who would be his friend. I asked for someone Alan would think was cool. I asked that this friend come alongside him and encourage him and help him to stay accountable and be an example of life as a man of God. I again cried during this prayer of pleading on bended knee in our family room.

Going through this pain and sharing more with Alan, he confessed of more than one affair in our marriage as he tried to come clean. This one riddled me, too. Since I had forgiven him of the one I caught him in, I felt I needed to forgive this other one that had been before. This one was even harder.

The rejection and deception that was in half of our marriage was shattering. I felt my life had been a lie. I had not been all to him that he was to me. He was everything to me. He was to have been my source of love for the rest of my life.

I stood and stared in disbelief at the headboard of our bed. When my grandma had died, I was allowed to have her beautiful antique headboard. On it she had put a wooden plaque that reads, "I will never leave you, nor forsake you. Hebrews 13:5." It was the first Bible verse I had memorized when I learned to read as a little girl. I couldn't believe how Alan could forsake me. He went to sleep under that verse every night.

Finally, it hit me. Alan never said that to me. Jesus did. I began to see where I had placed my longing for an incredible love to come from the man I married instead of the Lord.

This new way of thinking began to change everything I felt for God. I began to see His perfect love. His never-ending love would never leave me or forsake me. He never packed a suitcase. He was always the one with me each and every day. I had always held Alan up in that high seat of respect and fulfillment when I should have had Jesus there instead.

I started making changes. I became aware of myself in other ways. I started to take care of myself better. I got rid of my old fashioned granny panties. I exercised. I listened to worship songs as I worked out. Amazingly I was falling in love with Jesus in a whole new way as I noticed His hand constantly in my life. Love songs became about Jesus. The Bible was filled in Hosea, Jeremiah, Ezekiel, Daniel and more of God's jealousy and heartbreak over His beloved Israel as He compared her to an adulterer.

I grieved deeply, finally glimpsing the heartbreak of God as He watched His beloved betray Him. He had the same anger, the same pleading, the same forgiveness and longing for the love returned. I wept and prayed that His love would return to Him. This was the closest I had ever felt to Him. I was finally seeing that He is the greatest love of all.

Our daughter's marriage took place. Her husband was all I had prayed for those many years before from when she was a child in my womb and onto adulthood. Now, I prayed for her and her marriage in new ways. She was marrying a man who loved the Lord. They had kept their relationship before Him. I put my hope in Jesus for their marriage as I sat, still straining in my own marriage. We sat as husband and wife holding our two-year-old son as our lovely daughter said, “I do.” The church was full.

Despite my stronger faith in God, my faith in Alan was gone. I was resentful. I made sarcastic comments to try to offset my pain. I wouldn’t let him forget for a minute what he did and that I was checking on him. Bitterness has a stranglehold of roots that chokes out love. Bitterness is evidence of unforgiveness.

Chapter 10

Battle

"Open my eyes to the things You want me to see," was a common prayer as the year went on. We spent Alan's lunch hour together every day. We read from a devotion book for couples during the lunch break and in warm weather we would follow it up with a walk. These were things that Alan knew made me happy.

But things weren't completely better. He still enjoyed joking with the waitresses. I wondered if he did it for attention or as a way of flirting. If it was a male waiter, it didn't happen as much. He liked to make girls laugh and a lot of girls played into it too. They liked the attention as much as he did.

My jealousy stung, so did my mistrust. I remembered how he lured me with his sense of humor. I had hoped to see more changes in him, more self-control—or at least notice that I was hurting while he made light with other women. He didn't notice. If I said something, I felt like I was nagging. I wanted to be the one he would focus on and do his best to bring joy. I know I shot dirty looks at these women. What was worse was that I had been one of them. It was that part that helped me forgive them for not knowing what they did. I wasn't any better.

Reading in Proverbs, I found my perfect teaching scripture! There it was in black and white! I read it to Alan, trying to drill it home. I read it to other women

I knew. It became a battle cry. I even vowed to instill it in our son's heart when he was old enough.

Proverbs 6:20-7:27 (NLT):

My son, obey your father's commands, and
don't neglect your mother's instruction.[21] Keep their
words always in your heart. Tie them around your
neck.[22] When you walk, their counsel will lead you.
When you sleep, they will protect you. When you
wake up, they will advise you.[23] For their command is
a lamp and their instruction a light; their corrective
discipline is the way to life.[24] It will keep you from the
immoral woman, from the smooth tongue of a promis-
cuous woman.[25] Don't lust for her beauty. Don't let her
coy glances seduce you.[26] For a prostitute will bring
you to poverty, but sleeping with another man's wife
will cost you your life.[27] Can a man scoop a flame into
his lap and not have his clothes catch on fire?[28] Can
he walk on hot coals and not blister his feet?[29] So
it is with the man who sleeps with another man's
wife. He who embraces her will not go unpunished.
[30] Excuses might be found for a thief who steals be-
cause he is starving.[31] But if he is caught, he must
pay back seven times what he stole, even if he has to
sell everything in his house.[32] But the man who com-
mits adultery is an utter fool, for he destroys him-
self.[33] He will be wounded and disgraced. His shame
will never be erased.[34] For the woman's jealous hus-
band will be furious, and he will show no mercy when
he takes revenge.[35] He will accept no compensation,
nor be satisfied with a payoff of any size.

[1] Follow my advice, my son; always trea-
sure my commands.[2] Obey my commands and
live! Guard my instructions as you guard your
own eyes. [3] Tie them on your fingers as a re-
minder. Write them deep within your heart.
[4] Love wisdom like a sister; make insight a be-

loved member of your family.[5] Let them protect
you from an affair with an immoral woman, from
listening to the flattery of a promiscuous woman.
[6] While I was at the window of my house, look-
ing through the curtain,[7] I saw some naive young
men, and one in particular who lacked common
sense.[8] He was crossing the street near the house
of an immoral woman, strolling down the path by
her house.[9] It was at twilight, in the evening, as
deep darkness fell.[10] The woman approached him,
seductively dressed and sly of heart.[11] She was
the brash, rebellious type, never content to stay
at home.[12] She is often in the streets and markets,
soliciting at every corner.[13] She threw her arms
around him and kissed him, and with a brazen look
she said,[14] "I've just made my peace offerings and
fulfilled my vows.[15] You're the one I was looking for!
I came out to find you, and here you are![16] My bed is
spread with beautiful blankets, with colored sheets
of Egyptian linen.[17] I've perfumed my bed with
myrrh, aloes, and cinnamon.[18] Come, let's drink
our fill of love until morning. Let's enjoy each other's
caresses,[19] for my husband is not home. He's away
on a long trip.[20] He has taken a wallet full of money
with him and won't return until later this month. "
[21] So she seduced him with her pretty speech and
enticed him with her flattery.[22] He followed her at
once, like an ox going to the slaughter. He was like
a stag caught in a trap,[23] awaiting the arrow that
would pierce its heart. He was like a bird flying into
a snare, little knowing it would cost him his life.
[24] So listen to me, my sons, and pay attention to my
words.[25] Don't let your hearts stray away toward
her. Don't wander down her wayward path.[26] For
she has been the ruin of many; many men have
been her victims.[27] Her house is the road to the
grave. Her bedroom is the den of death.

I believed that Alan no longer had any conversations or relationship with the other woman, but my eyes were opened. I learned he still talked with her. I felt I had been betrayed again. This time I couldn't contain it.

In a blur of reaction, I fled in fear of being trapped in a cage of lies. I told him to come home and that I needed some time away. He was to watch our son because I didn't know what I was going to do. I also gave him clear instructions: It was time he told our daughters what had been going on. They would notice I wasn't home and it was because of him. I was forcing him to man up to the consequences and start doing the explaining.

I nervously packed a little bag. I had never threatened to leave before and I had never taken such strong actions against my husband in stepping away from our home emotionally or physically. I grabbed my purse and my Bible and went to a nearby motel. I was so mad and I didn't want to do anything rash. I kept begging the Lord to keep me in the center of His hand and in the center of His will. *Please, Lord, don't let me go to the left or to the right, forward or backward, but keep me in Your will.*

Alan asked me when I was coming back. I said that I didn't know. He adamantly told me he was not having a physical relationship with her. But, to me it was still a relationship. It was also happening without me knowing about it. I felt I was still being deceived.

Prayers, tears, and reading the Bible filled my night in the motel. It was the first time in my life I'd been in a motel room by myself, but, I did not feel alone. Jesus pressed in and was there in scripture and in my pounding, screaming heart. He managed to keep me focused on Him and my desire to please Him overtook my own need to retaliate.

I didn't want our son to suffer without me there. I knew my girls were hearing painful things and I wasn't there to comfort them. They sent me text messages asking if I was okay. I knew I needed to go home the next morning. It was where I belonged.

I wrote a list of the things that I did not like in his character. I wrote the way I wanted to be treated and what I dreamed of in a marriage. After nervously arriving home, Alan decided he needed to leave for a while. This wasn't good. He decided to stay away for several days. I never got to show him my list. I tore it up because I couldn't even stand to read what I had written about his character. It was ugly and my heart wouldn't let me put it out there no matter how badly I was hurt.

Our girls came home and cried with me. My tears were tears for them too. Their life had been shattered, like mine, in learning what they believed to be our family, really wasn't. What was worse for them was that they had no control. As the children, your hands are tied. All that they could do was pray. The sin trickled into the family. Sin is far reaching. Sin causes pain to so many innocent people. It spreads and spoils and destroys. I sat helplessly hurting and waiting to hear from Alan.

When he returned he said he would look for a place to live. I said I didn't want him to leave. I wanted him to stay in our house. It would be good for Sam to still have him near. I also wanted him near. I didn't want this family broken. I wanted it fixed. I had no idea how to fix it.

He moved his things downstairs. My heart wrenched as I watched him. His face was cold and hard as he kept his eyes only on what he was doing and never once looked up at me. He was angry and frustrated. He'd given up.

Begging for a miracle, for an answer to "why" this was happening, I reached out to my mom and shared what was happening. I needed more prayers. I needed more support. I couldn't go at this on my own anymore. I couldn't bear to be the one to tell my dad. She told him for me. I was seeing the situation as desperate, so I finally opened up and shared it. I needed help. I asked for prayers, I asked for prayers for the children, for prayers for Alan, for prayers for guidance and for prayers for God's will.

My parents too, were brokenhearted. They loved Alan. They loved me. They loved our children and yet, they knew our children needed a godly father. That became their prayer.

The awkwardness of living together and keeping our son feeling secure without really having anything under our feet was exhausting. We would have moments of discussion. Alan seemed to not want to be the one to say it was over and did his best to make me say it. He told me he didn't know if he could be faithful to me a year from now, six months from now or days from now. I don't know how I managed to take another breath.

He again said he would never be like me. He would never be the way I wished he was. He would never pray like me or talk about the Lord like I do. He had stopped coming to church because again, he said that he only ever went for me. He looked different to me. He looked hard, lines on his face were deep and his eyes were cold.

We were to have family photos taken for our church directory. I pleaded for him to still go with us. In my mind, I believed it would probably be our last family photo together and at least our little boy would be able to flip through the book and see us together.

As we posed for the photos, it was exactly that, just a pose. Even the leaning in or placing a hand on him felt like I was touching a stranger. I didn't know the man anymore and yet Jesus kept me holding on to the marriage.

Chapter 11

The Battle Belongs to Him

Looking for Jesus to give me some direction, any direction, I prayed and cried out. My body returned to the wrenching of worry and fear as I could not keep food down. As soon as my mind went to the place of deception I would gag and shake.

One morning I woke with a scripture passage spoken clearly to me. I had never received scripture direction audibly before from Him. I got up and went into the porch and read Philippians 4:1-8. Verse seven says, "If you do this, you will experience God's peace, which is far more wonderful than the human mind can understand. His peace will guard your hearts and minds as you live in Christ Jesus." I knew I was to guard my heart against bitterness. To try and stay in His peace even though it felt like the vision of my life was gone. I was to forgive another woman and I was to dwell on the things that were good and beautiful. It was a tall order. Some of it was easier than others as I battled the uncertainty and looming loss of my husband. That fear still shot through my heart like a spear.

My parents reached out to other family members for prayer for us. My aunt, who works with grief support through their funeral home, sent me a small pink blanket with silk trim. She remembered that I had been a "blankie" girl when I was little. When I opened the package I giggled a little and I put that blanket up inside my shirt all wadded up over my heart. The silk and softness touched my real aching heart that pained with every heartbeat. I took this gift with me in bed too, under my pajama top, as I slept alone. God works in unusual ways and her sensitivity in what I was going through was equal to loss and grief. Her gift brought physical comfort to an also physical pain. It was sweet, tender, and comforting as I felt as vulnerable as a child.

She was also an example of forgiveness and great strength. She clung to her marriage through my uncle's suffering with a bi-polar condition. She loved him, protected him and their home and business by leaning on Jesus through all of it. When his health was restored, their marriage sparkled. The problems had become victories and testimonies of what God did. This was hope. Theirs were prayers of understanding and pleadings for the same mercies in our marriage.

I tried to think of ways of how to work through the nightmare I was living. I prayed on hands and knees. I prayed while laying on the floor or curled in a ball. I prayed with my face buried between tear-soaked hands. Prayng as I did, I would try to hear from the Lord what I was to do next. I couldn't hear anything. The pain was deafening. The sharpness was loudness. I couldn't hear past my screaming heart. I kept begging to be in the center of God's will. I pictured myself as a tiny mustard seed in the center of His perfect palm. I wasn't even thinking of the representation of it being faith. I just thought of how very small a mustard seed was.

One afternoon, my mom called and said she was going to come over. She said she had been in prayer and the Lord shared something with her. I couldn't wait for her to arrive. Finally, some peace, some direction, and some comfort. She came in and sat down. Her expression was serious. I strained forward, waiting to hear what she had to say. She told me, "Lori, God said He's using Alan to draw you closer to Him." "WHAT?!" I exclaimed, "But, this hurts so BAD!" She looked as confused by it as I was. How could this be? I clutched my blankie-filled shirt. It wasn't the freeing of pain that I thought it was going to be. It wasn't the direction that I was hoping to receive. At the very least, I thought that maybe the Lord might even say that He was going to smite Alan for me. Nope, God was using Alan. This trial had purpose. By God's permissive will, He was going to use it for good.

I couldn't argue. I had come closer to Him. I had to. Who I had become dependent on for love, security, and value was no longer there. I had to learn that those things come from the Lord. I couldn't depend on a person for it. I hadn't been valuing the Lord for those things. Now I was learning how to—the hard way.

As another day ended, I went to bed alone. I turned the television on in the bedroom and switched the channel to some Christian broadcasting. I continually searched for any sort of comfort. As I turned, there was one of my favorite Bible teachers, Beth Moore. I had fallen in love with that little half-pint from Texas and I was thrilled to have found her on TV. I had only attended DVD Bible studies of hers and read some books. There she was lighting up my darkened bedroom as the Lord showed me what to do next.

The message was the teaching of 2 Chronicles 20. The main point of the message is "The battle belongs to the Lord." Verse by verse, the instructions of a battle that in no way could be humanly won was handled by the Lord. I was in a battle that I could not possibly compete in and win. My enemy was younger, beautiful, and available each and every day. I felt completely unequipped to win. As I read the scriptures I began to pray them into my life. It was my life.

This scripture prayed into your life is the strongest weapon you could ever have in any battle.

> 11b "For they have come to throw us out of your land, which you gave us as an inheritance.[12] O our God, won't you stop them? We are powerless against this mighty army that is about to attack us. We do not know what to do, but we are looking to you for help."[13] As all the men of Judah stood before the LORD with their little ones, wives, and children,[14] the Spirit of the LORD came upon one of the men standing there. His name was Jahaziel son of Zechariah, son of Benaiah, son of Jeiel, son of Mattaniah, a Levite who was a descendant of Asaph.[15] He said, "Listen, all you people of Judah and Jerusalem! Listen, King Jehoshaphat! This is what the LORD says: Do not be afraid! Don't be discouraged by this mighty army, for the battle is not yours, but God's.[16] Tomorrow, march out against them. You will find them coming up through the ascent of Ziz at the end of the valley that opens into the wilderness of Jeruel.[17] But you will not even need to fight. Take your positions; then stand still and watch the LORD's victory. He is with you, O people of Judah and Jerusalem. Do not be afraid or discouraged. Go out against them tomorrow, for the LORD is with you!"[18] Then King Jehoshaphat bowed low with his face to the ground. And all the people of Judah and Jerusalem did the same, worshiping the LORD.[19] Then the Levites from the clans of Kohath and Korah stood to praise the LORD, the God of Israel, with a very loud shout.[20] Early the next morning the army of Judah went out into the wilderness of Tekoa. On the way Jehoshaphat

stopped and said, "Listen to me, all you people of Judah and Jerusalem! Believe in the LORD your God, and you will be able to stand firm. Believe in his prophets, and you will succeed."[21] After consulting the people, the king appointed singers to walk ahead of the army, singing to the LORD and praising him for his holy splendor. This is what they sang:

"Give thanks to the LORD; his faithful love endures forever!"

[22] At the very moment they began to sing and give praise, the LORD caused the armies of Ammon, Moab, and Mount Seir to start fighting among themselves.[23] The armies of Moab and Ammon turned against their allies from Mount Seir and killed every one of them. After they had destroyed the army of Seir, they began attacking each other.[24] So when the army of Judah arrived at the lookout point in the wilderness, all they saw were dead bodies lying on the ground as far as they could see. Not a single one of the enemy had escaped.[25] King Jehoshaphat and his men went out to gather the plunder. They found vast amounts of equipment, clothing, and other valuables—more than they could carry. There was so much plunder that it took them three days just to collect it all![26] On the fourth day they gathered in the Valley of Blessing, which got its name that day because the people praised and thanked the LORD there. It is still called the Valley of Blessing today.[27] Then all the men returned to Jerusalem, with Jehoshaphat leading them, overjoyed that the LORD had given them victory over their enemies.[28] They marched into Jerusalem to the music of harps, lyres, and trumpets, and they proceeded to the Temple of the LORD.[29] When all the surrounding kingdoms heard that the LORD himself had fought against the ene-

> mies of Israel, the fear of God came over them.[30] So Jehoshaphat's kingdom was at peace, for his God had given him rest on every side."
> 2 Chronicles 20:11-30 (NLT)

I didn't need to fight! What I did have to fight was fear. The praising helps put the Lord in His rightful place on the throne of power and holiness in our hearts. Just as the people were told to sing and praise, I too, did it. Sometimes the only song I could even utter through the surging lump in my throat was "Holy, Holy, Holy," as I would drop to my knees in times of grief.

Our daughters were praying before the Lord for their dad, our little three-year-old Samuel was praying for his dad too, just as it said in verse thirteen of standing before the Lord with their wives, children, and little ones. We stood before the Lord. Our daughter, Kristin, was working at Mt. Carmel, a Christian camp in Alexandria, Minnesota. She had them praying for our family too.

My aunt, who had sent the blanket, sent more messages of their prayers for us. One even said they were praying with their "faces to the ground." She did not know the scripture that I was praying and claiming for our family as the verse reads, "[18] Then King Jehoshaphat bowed low with his face to the ground. And all the people of Judah and Jerusalem did the same, worshiping the LORD."

The scripture says to show up, but that you don't need to fight. "Instead, take your positions and stand still and **watch** the Lord's victory."

Praising and singing through the trials, I have learned, is an outward expression of faith. It is faith externalized. It is the expectation that in all things

He is good and mighty. That expectation is faith as you believe in Him that He will come through.

Still, the inner turmoil raged. I saw myself as old. I loathed what age did to my skin. During a night of mentally tearing myself apart in front of a mirror and feeling completely out of control, the Lord SANG! He imitated James Blunt and sang the words from one of his songs. He sang this portion, "You're beautiful to me." He used the same voice, the same note fluctuation and vibrato that James Blunt does. I started laughing! It struck me so funny! The voice came out of nowhere and in no way had I been thinking those words. I was thinking "ugly." Tears started to fill my eyes and roll down my cheeks. I never thought the Lord may sing to me. I never thought He'd imitate someone, but why not?! He created that voice! Our sweet, precious Lord did that!!! He tore me away from hating myself because He saw me as beautiful. He did it with humor and love. He did it the way I am moved. He moved me. He wooed me. He loved me and I went to sleep at peace that night. I pray that this is a glimpse into the heart of our Lord for you.

I am nothing special. I am someone who loves Him, and believes in Him. That is all and that is all it takes. This is what He will do for you, for any of you. Maybe it was because I had been singing to Him, even though it was difficult, I don't know. But He loves you and to Him, you are beautiful. He will move you and woo you the way that you are moved. He knows your heart.

Chapter 12

Bended Knees

He sees the end from the beginning and the beginning from the end. Imagination could never have come up with what was to come. I knew that Jesus was with me. I knew whatever was going to happen, He was going to take care of me. The boat I was on was in treacherous waters, but Jesus, too, was in the boat.

As people were reaching out in prayer, our pastor was calling and talking with me, too. He offered to talk with Alan and I told him to if he felt led. I was hopeful and I prayed that Jesus would soften Alan enough to want to talk with him.

Alan said yes, he would meet with him. I was elated! I had so much hope that he was looking for help. I prayed during that meeting. When he returned he seemed a little bit happier. He was talking to me more and I thanked the Lord.

After dinner that night, Alan told me he was going to the health club to work out. A little later, our son wanted to see his dad and was fussing about it. I packed Sam up and went to the health club. Usually when we are at the health club together, Alan will play with Sam in the gym after his workout.

We pulled into the parking lot and I quickly saw that his car wasn't there. I decided to go inside anyway and work out and let Sam play with the children in the child care area. I was upset, and pounding on a treadmill helped me burn up some of that anger. I was also afraid.

A woman who worked in the child care area came up to me and said that my son had fallen and hit his head pretty hard and that he was crying for his dad. I went to Sam right away and I tried calling Alan. He didn't answer. I left a message about what had happened and that Sam was hurting and wanted him. We went home and I put Sam in pajamas and kept an eye on him.

An hour or so later, Alan came home and was covered in sweat like he had been working out. I asked him where he had been and he said he was working out. Then he told me he went to another health club with the girl and her family because she and her sister had invited him to their club for a "Friends and Family" event.

That was it. I couldn't do it anymore. All that I had hoped and prayed, all the new hope I had earlier in the afternoon because he was meeting with a pastor, was gone. It didn't matter. He had made his plans. I took off my wedding rings, slammed them on the dresser and said, "You chose your family tonight." I told him it was over. I told him to get out. I took a stand for righteousness. I was not going to allow myself to be deceived anymore.

The anger felt good. I finally had control of something. I didn't know what tomorrow was going to bring, but I knew it would be with the Lord. I didn't care where Alan went. After twenty years of caring where he was and how he was and wanting the best for him, that was the first night I didn't.

Continuing to take care of Sam and still doing real estate through all of the days of turmoil before, I got up and started another day. A real estate agent I was working with on a transaction called my cell phone. She wanted to schedule an inspection on a house that I was representing before the final purchase was made. She'd left a message requesting the inspection.

I returned her call and she didn't answer so I began to leave her a message. "Hi, Mary, this is Lori. Yes, it is fine for you to go through the house. The lockbox combination is 7 0..." and then I broke down bawling. I couldn't get the last number out of my mouth. I sputtered and sniffed and told her, "I'm sorry, I think my marriage just ended. I know you are a Christian woman, please pray for me." *Click.* I hung up the phone. I could not believe what had just happened. I was humiliated. I knew she believed in Jesus. There had been signs. The people she was representing in purchasing the home were missionaries who had finished their work and were buying their very first home. She also advertised at times using Christian symbols. But, ugh! I had lost absolute professionalism and control.

Thirty minutes later my phone rang. It was Mary. I was way too embarrassed to even answer it. I just let it ring. She left a message. I finally brought myself to listen to her message. Her very first words were, "Lori, this is my ministry, I work with couples in crisis." My mouth hung open. She went on to describe how she works, all in the name of Jesus, and comes right into our home. "We talk with one another and talk very straight forward and start to peel back some of the layers of what is being done. I meet you and I meet Alan right at your level."

I knew. I knew I had to allow this. I knew that God made this whole thing happen. Mary's phone call was from Him and I had to obey and listen to her. When Alan came by to see Sam I let him listen to the message. I asked Alan if he would meet with Mary. He told me that he didn't know and that he would need to think about it. All of a sudden I felt out of control again. I desperately wanted him to say yes.

Our daughter, Kristin, who was working at Mt. Carmel Ministries called me. She said the people who run the camp wanted to invite me, Sam and my daughter, Kendra and her husband Sam up for a time to all be together. I knew this would be good for Kristin because she wasn't able to be here to help support and love like she would have liked. I also thought it would be good for me to get away.

I told Alan we were going up there for four days. I asked if he had an answer yet about meeting with Mary. He said he didn't but that he would when I got back. I told him to come back and stay in our house while we were gone.

Leaving for camp was scary. I felt like I had to be strong for the kids and make sure they had fun. It ended up that I didn't have to do a thing. We enjoyed the lake, a cozy cabin, wonderful food, and each other. It was peaceful, loving, and filled with joy. The camp organizers had speakers and song leaders. They hosted funny events and all kinds of water playtime and Bible study activities.

I was being fed in my heart and in my body. What had still been a struggle for me to even cook or face much of eating was being lovingly prepared for me. It was delicious food and it filled me and stayed with me. I was feeling so much stronger. They prayed with me and for me and for the whole family.

Down low at the water's edge stood a small building. It looked as if maybe one day it had been a fish cleaning hut. Now it had a small wooden cross at the top of its peak. The small structure was painted white with light blue trim like most of the cabins at the camp. Its windows were all screens. Above the narrow door was a rustic sign that read, “Prayer Chapel.”

Sam and I took the steep, stone path down to the small chapel. We went inside and found chairs and a kneeling board with Bibles and prayer cards on a ledge. Samuel and I kneeled side by side. We prayed for his daddy, we asked that his daddy would know and love Jesus like we do and that he would know how much Jesus loved him. Sam’s small folded hands and bowed head were held with the deepest sincerity.

Getting up, I gave him a hug and we walked along the water’s edge. We threw some stones and headed back up to the lodge. The camp was a family camp. Families filled the cabins, events were planned as couples had Bible time and the kids joined other kids. At mealtime, the families regrouped or would go on to private time together.

I watched the couples. I watched them with their children as they shared their time together. This was their family vacation. They chose to spend it at a family Bible camp. As I watched the interaction, it all seemed like a different world. I couldn’t imagine studying the Bible with my husband or praying together with other couples and families. I couldn’t imagine him ever having fun with people like this. I saw their joy, their play, and their peacefulness with one another.

Kristin got to interact with families week after week as they came and went. When she was younger she had asked if we could go to family camp with our church. I told her “no” because dad probably wouldn’t like it. Another family talked about taking her as an “adopted” member. Later, the church became more direct in their desire that people come as families. She didn’t go again. Now she was able to work at a camp like this and be a part of it all summer long. I was so happy for her. The people who ran it loved her like one of their own. They were also loving me and all of my children, and praying for my marriage.

That evening the speaker opened up by saying that he has become known as the "Disaster Pastor." He was speaking in Fargo, North Dakota when the terrible flood came. He was called down to Louisiana immediately following Hurricane Katrina. As he spoke, he told of the spinning of our world, our solar system, our galaxy and the very atoms in our bodies. All spinning and held in place. He said that sometimes our lives seem to be spinning out of control but know that God is holding it all in place. He is there and He is keeping it together.

The message was another blanket of comfort. Then, he picked up a guitar quite unexpectedly, because he had not finished the message. He slowly started to pick out some notes and held them into the other. Then he started to sing in a low voice. He sang, "There is peace like a river in my soul." Over and over he slowly sang this. Every time he sang it, he sang it louder until the thin shell that I had become, cracked. Again my eyes filled to brimming as tears poured down my face. My shoulders shook and my tightened throat could no longer hold in my breath as it gushed out in a staccato exhale. My sobbing was air, in and out. No one said anything. My nose ran, my face reddened as I sputtered through breaths. The pastor looked out at me. He may have prayed within his heart, and I'm sure others around me may have prayed. But, it wasn't visible. I sat there, alone amongst the couples, but I felt like I was a couple too. I was sitting with Jesus and He was letting me know He was holding everything together. I felt peace like a river in my soul and I felt loved.

During the quiet time I sat by the lake and read my Bible and wrote notes. I didn't know what God had planned. I didn't know if He had someone else in mind for me one day. I wrote down the things I would love to have in a man, the things that I would look for differently.

As I packed up, I was at peace. I was full physically and spiritually. I was ready to face Alan's answer about meeting with Mary. He would say yes or no and either way, I was going to be okay. I hoped for his sake that he would say yes and take a shot at knowing Jesus. God had knocked with that phone call and I knew we needed to answer it.

Chapter 13

A Mighty Wind

Driving back home was harder than I had imagined. As I got further from camp and closer to home, I knew my answers to what was coming next. I kept Sam cheerful in the back seat as we talked about our favorite parts of the camp and our favorite things that we did. Having to do that helped me not to dwell entirely on what was ahead. I still held on to hope for things to be better.

Pulling into the driveway, I was nervous, but excited. I expected Alan to jump up and open the door or help me carry in our cases and things. He barely looked up. He didn't get up. He quietly said, "Hi" to Sam. He wouldn't understand anything of what I'd just experienced. It was a world he'd never known. I didn't bother to tell him anything about it, other than letting him know that Kristin sends her love as I hoisted our cases back inside the house myself.

Once Sam was busy and settled, I took a deep breath and I walked over to Alan and asked him what his decision was about meeting with Mary. He'd had four days of quiet to really ponder everything and I was ready for a "yes" or a "no." He said, "I don't know yet."

That unexpected answer infuriated me. How could he not know?! I asked him in a sneering way, "Did you even *think* about it while we were gone?" He told me, "Not really." It seemed as if everything was getting worse. To me it felt like a "No." He wasn't going to meet with Mary, which I realized was not okay with me. I also felt even more neglected. I made my own assumptions because I had also set my own expectations and they weren't met. While my entire time away was consumed with what was happening in our marriage, he said he hadn't really thought about it. I felt like I had wasted my life.

I stomped around, cried some more, acted indignant and cried out to God, "Why didn't you give me the t-shirt boy?!" (This was the boy from my first date who sold t-shirts at Alan's soccer games.) Life would have been simpler all the way around. I was sure that I wouldn't have had all I'd had to endure. He surely would have been kinder. He wouldn't have treated me like this. It was then that I realized all that I thought was so wonderful about Alan's life—his fame and achievement—didn't matter anymore.

Once evening came and I settled down again, I brought myself back to asking to be in the center of God's will. I prayed again for a godly father for Samuel and for His love and comfort for our children. I prayed blessings on all of the people at Mt. Carmel and for continued blessings and anointing on their ministry. I prayed again, for Alan, too.

The next day I talked again with Alan about he and I doing our best for our children. I told him I would never keep him from being with our kids and I would always want him to be a part of their lives. I told him I knew how important he was in their lives and that they loved him very much.

Friends and family who were aware of my actions could not believe how I was able to do it. I have to say, I would never think that I could keep the kindness up in such a situation. It is only by the grace of God.

Friends have suffered losses, such as a missing child and other tragedies, and I have seen them hold together in unimaginable strength and grace. I believe God gives us the grace that we need at the time. It is a way of seeing His glory, because what we walk through would consume us to hatred, anger, and building walls if we weren't walking with Him. A devotional titled *Reflections of the Heart of God* by Roy Lessin says, "A heart that receives from God has so many riches to give to others." It is nothing that we do, it is what He does to us.

As I let go of Alan more and more with every rejection, I knew I would be okay. But, I never stopped wanting Alan to know Jesus. He needed Him. He was living a life of hell on earth without Him, not to mention the eternity. Everything seemed dark before me. I didn't know what my future would be, since my past had been emptied and my present was pain, me, and Jesus. But I still had hope of a better life—the Lord promised it. Psalm 30:5 (NLT) says, "For his anger lasts only a moment, but his favor lasts a lifetime! Weeping may last through the night, but joy comes with the morning."

Saturday night came, and I went to bed alone as usual. I lay quietly, staring at the ceiling, and then I heard the Lord speak! I had never experienced anything like that before. It was loud! It was a proclamation, with the most words I'd ever heard strung together from Him. He said, "*Tomorrow there will be a rush like a mighty wind and it will befall a seed. Watch and see its yield.*" PEACE. I melted into the bed. Every muscle went soft, my heart quieted and my mind tingled in the calm. I felt as if I had sunk into a cloud of softness. I felt a peace like I had never felt before. I am certain, had I not been in bed, that I would have been faint and unable to stand, the muscles went that soft.

My mind held to the word "watch." There was nothing for me to do, only to watch. The sense of striving and clinging and fighting and working for Alan's salvation, love, and happiness was replaced with "watch." I slept sound and I woke with peace. I got ready for church and I got Sam ready.

Arriving earlier than usual, I went ahead and placed Sam in the nursery and I got my choice of places to sit in the sanctuary. I chose to sit closer up front than usual. I wanted to be closer to the cross before me and closer to the message giver. Not long after I sat down, my parents came in and sat next to me. They usually sat farther back, but they didn't want me to sit alone.

We sang our lovely contemporary songs accompanied by electric guitars, keyboards, and drums. It was peppy and we were praising. As we sat down after some brief words from the song leader, he said, "Open your hymnals." What?! A hymn during a contemporary service! This never happened. We had been singing for at least twenty minutes and now we were switching over to this.

It was a pretty song, slow, with many verses. As we sang we reached a verse and my eyes about popped out of my head as we sang the words, "Rush like a mighty wind." It was the same words spoken to me by the Lord the night before! Just as we sang that part, there stood Alan, alongside the pew I was sitting in! He had come to church! He hadn't been in months. He looked serious, he looked shaken, and he squeezed himself past my parents to get in next to me. I can't imagine how it was for Alan to see them for the first time since everything had happened. He had walked into the sanctuary well after it had started and walked clear to the front and physically had to brush past my parents to sit next to me at the exact time we were singing that part of the song! Only God!

I was shaking. I don't remember anything about the message. I knew God did this. What was He doing? After the service ended, Alan told me he would see me at home. I was in shock for what had just happened.

When I got home with Sam, Alan told me that he had been seated up in the balcony. He had felt like he needed to go to church that day. As he looked down from there, he saw me. He said he heard God say, "It's time to let her go." It scared him. He looked around and saw me surrounded by all of the people who were there and he said he knew I would be okay and that it would probably be the last time he would ever get to sit by me again. He was so shaken that he didn't care if he came in the middle of the service to sit by me one last time.

I listened to him. Then he said he wanted to meet with Mary! God did something to him. The rush of His mighty wind had made a seed fall. I couldn't really imagine God saying, "It's time to let her go." I wasn't sure it was really Him talking to Alan. We asked others and they said it must not have been God. Alan was angry and said, "Why is it that all of you can hear from God, but I can't?!" He was right and I decided to trust God that there was some purpose in it. It had certainly made him do things he would have never done.

I called Mary and told her Alan wanted to meet. This meeting to me was the chance for Alan to come to Jesus. Mary came in three days. We sat in our own family room. Mary sat in a wooden chair facing us, Alan sat on a couch, and I sat in an overstuffed chair.

Chapter 14

His Glory

Mary began talking. She shared with Alan what she knew about our situation. She thanked him for wanting to meet. She acknowledged how important that was and that she knew it was no small thing. She clearly said we are meeting all in the name of Jesus and made sure we understood that. We both nodded.

I told her the words that the Lord had spoken to me on Saturday night. She listened and wrote. I then told her how Alan came to church and he heard the words, "It's time to let her go." Without any hesitation she exclaimed, "That is exactly right!" She looked at Alan and said that it was time to let Lori go. She told him that his relationship with the Lord is between the two of them, not through Lori. "What has happened to Lori releases her from you," she said.

For the first time, I felt free. I no longer had the weight of trying to rescue Alan or us. I didn't have to. It was God's job. Alan was glued to Mary. She spoke to him in the same words he would use. She even cussed and she had his full attention. He was listening. He was answering back and he was open. He was open to a total stranger; a woman. A woman who was not defending him, but showing him what was and is for him.

As she asked Alan about himself and if he ever saw anyone do the things he did to me while he was growing up, he said he had. He shared stories I had never heard from his childhood. He cried at the memories and Mary pulled out tissues and handed them to him. I was silent and stunned.

She asked where he would go and what he did when things like that happened. He said he would run to his Grandma's. Mary lovingly told him that God never wanted him to have those things happen to him. God was there in the people he ran to, like Grandma, in a place for him to run. Alan was that broken child in front of me sobbing at the memories and the learning of God's love for him even in the midst of his suffering.

As she gently spoke, she then asked if He wanted the Lord who had always loved Him to be a part of His life. She asked if he wanted to be forgiven for all of the things that he had ever done. She told him how Jesus went to the cross for him and every sin, and that He rose again. She explained that Jesus is a gentleman and that He doesn't come uninvited. She told him that he had to ask Him. Alan nodded through the tears and got on his knees. He spoke the words out loud for Jesus to forgive him and to come into his life and change him. I sat in shock. My pain was still strong and my pain made me doubt.

As Alan asked Jesus into his life, he then turned to me in deep sorrow and said he was sorry. He laid his tear-soaked face on my lap and I could scarcely bring my hand to his head. Mary told me as he cried that he was feeling for the first time the pain that he caused. I was hard. I could hardly stand to have him touch me. I was as stuffed with bitterness and self-righteousness as the overstuffed chair in which I sat.

As he softened, I seemed to harden. Mary explained to him that for me, it was like I had seen my entire platoon blown up in front of me. Some soldiers are able to return to that place again, she explained, and some never go back. She told him that it would be up to me. She talked about me to him as I sat in their presence. Every word was right.

Alan was feeling better. He said it felt like a weight had been taken off him that had been so great and until it was gone he had no idea he had been carrying it. Mary asked him if he would be willing to meet with her and some other prayer people to continue to strip back the layers of the things in his life that needed more healing. He said he would do anything to feel better and to try and make our marriage right. Again, I sat in shock. My mouth was wide open.

Alan was changing in front of me. He was doing things I never thought he would. He was agreeable, he was thankful for being saved by Jesus, by being forgiven by Jesus. He was sorry.

Around the house Alan was hopeful. He kept trying to talk to me. He was the one chasing me. I continued to pray and asked God to keep me in His will. I didn't want to do anything He didn't want me to do. I remembered what He said, "Watch and see its yield." I just had to keep watching for the "fruits." The fruits would be my evidence of a true change.

Shortly, the arrangements were made for Alan to go and meet for prayer and the "peeling back of layers." He asked me to drive him there. Sam was in the backseat. We pulled up. I said a quick prayer that God would continue to help Alan. In he walked, into a home with strangers where he would share all that needed fixing, all that was broken and all of the places that he needed Jesus. This willing man was not the same man I married.

I prayed a lot during that afternoon. I played with Sam when I needed a distraction. A few hours later, my phone rang. Alan was ready for me to pick him up. His voice was softer and it was lighter.

Pulling into the driveway, he opened the door and stepped out. He was glowing—I mean, really glowing! He had a white light all over his face and head! He was smiling. I knew what I was seeing! I was seeing the presence of God. I couldn't handle it! It was like seeing Charlton Heston, who played Moses in The Ten Commandments, coming down from the mountain. I was seeing the white presence of the Lord on the face of the person who had become my enemy. I was torn in two. The conflict of my mind and my heart was more than I could handle. I told Alan I was going to drop him off at the house with Sam and I needed to get away.

This was more than I ever expected or was ready to comprehend. It was all I had ever dreamed or prayed! But I couldn't stand it. God had given me a glow-in-the-dark husband and I was still mad!!! As I drove, trying not to look at Alan, he told me he knew he was going to be okay. He said whatever I decided to do, that he would be okay, because now he has Jesus. Even as I write this, I have to stop and let this soak in again. He said what?!

After dropping him off, I went to the Mall of America. I thought I would look for blouses to put that out of my mind for a while, but as I pushed the tops along the racks, all I could think of was Alan's glowing face. I attempted to escape it for over an hour, but it wasn't happening. I decided to go back home.

There he sat—happy, content, and radiant. I couldn't pour out anger on this new Alan anymore because he was changed. I was frustrated because I couldn't lash out at the enemy in my pain. Then Alan told me more of what had happened that afternoon.

As they were praying over him, one of the women had a vision. Alan told me that she said, "I see Alan as a child and Jesus is standing in front of him facing him and Jesus is wearing a miner's hat and the light is shining on Alan." Alan said, "There was no way she could have known anything about me. My dad was a coal miner and his father before that was a coal miner and as far back as I know they were coal miners!" Jesus had stood in the gap of the generational sins that had followed his family. I began believing more strongly that what had happened to Alan had really happened. Jesus was making him new.

Mary called me and asked how I was doing. She asked about Alan, too. She recommended that we attend a conference coming at a local church nearby. It was called the Holy Spirit Conference. She said there were a lot of classes on marriage repair as well as other wonderful teaching. It went for a few days. I asked Alan if he wanted to go and he instantly said yes. Again, I was shocked. Two weeks later, the conference started.

We arrived at this huge church. It was like a convention. There were all sorts of vendors and classes, and people were all so friendly and happy. Alan was just as cheery. I felt God pushing me toward staying in the marriage or at least making His will crystal clear.

Friday night there was a national speaker who came. Things were happening that I had never experienced and neither had Alan. The room held 2500 people or more. They were singing, beach balls were being bounced in the air, and children and adults were waving flags of every color. It was a celebration praising God.

As the speaker got up and spoke, he had a soft gentle voice. He was funny and very down to earth.

He shared about miracles he had witnessed of God's healing and power. It was incredible. Alan was fixed on him.

As he continued talking it came to a time for prayer. He asked if anyone in the group had back pain or back problems and asked them to stand. Alan stood up. He then said for the people around those who were standing to place their hands on them and pray together for their healing. We prayed. Alan exclaimed, "It's gone! My back is fine!"

Other prayer requests were made and people were being healed all around us. He then asked who would like the gift of tongues, a prayer language of the Holy Spirit, to raise their hands. Alan raised his hand! Again, my eyes and mouth showed shock. As those who had raised their hands were instructed to quietly pray to themselves, the speaker prayed that the Holy Spirit would come and give the gift. Alan didn't even know what it was! But, he was signing up for it! He received it.

I could not deny what God was doing with Alan. I saw the changes, I saw the yields. Yet, my heart still hurt. I had a sharp pain that still existed even physically. I couldn't fight the truth of the change in Alan. I knew God wanted us together. He had worked a miracle in him. I figured if I went back to Alan it would be at my expense. It would glorify God, it would be good for the children but I would have to suffer with living with the memory of it every day. Yet, I saw the lengths the Lord was going for Alan. I saw Alan happy and enjoying his personal party with the Holy Spirit. I could either join him or continue to sit in the pain and bitterness of my heart.

So, sitting in my auditorium chair, I quietly closed my eyes and bowed my head. I said, "Okay, Lord. I will stay with him, but please take this pain from my heart and help me to love him." As I prayed this I touched my heart. In that instant of prayer, the pain left my heart. The sharpness that felt like razor blades with every beat of my heart was gone! Then, a love poured over me and into me. It was physically warm feeling, peaceful, and joyful. I reached my hand to Alan and he held it and we both were filled with joy.

When the service ended, we walked out to the car hand in hand. It was a beginning. It was new and fresh and I felt like a teenager in love. Only Jesus could have brought this. Only Jesus could have taken that pain in an instant and replaced it with love. Only Jesus could have changed a man in front of my very eyes.

Driving home, we were giggling like children on Christmas. We talked about the things that we saw that night—God's hand on so many and the healings. Alan spoke about the gift of the Holy Spirit and how his tongue started moving and making sounds that he didn't know. He was astounded and had never known anything like it. He never saw it in a church before, he never even heard of it, and yet, the Lord gave it to him at his request. Even with him not knowing what he asked for, the Lord gave.

As Alan spoke in excitement, he turned to me and said, "I'm like you! I want to talk about God all of the time!" The words that had fought me all of our married life—him saying he would never be like me and would never talk about God like I do—had been changed. God showed me what He had done to the man for whom I had prayed all of those years. I had stayed in my marriage and had entrusted God with that man. Those words were more precious to me than any treasure on earth and they spouted out of him like a fountain!

Chapter 15

Hand in Hand

We were like newlyweds. We started to do things together and even had someone look after Sam so that we could be together alone as a couple. It was good for us and it was good for Sam, too.

Alan took me to the Malt Shop, a local Minneapolis favorite and icon. As we sipped our malts and waited for our dinner to arrive, he looked at me. His eyes sparkled with the light that only the Lord can put into one's eyes. He was looking at me as if it were the first time. He commented on my beauty and he said I was radiant. He sat in amazement of ME. There was a love that came from him that was fully complete. He was seeing all of me, inside and out. For the first time, he knew me. He recognized my heart, the Spirit inside and the beauty that comes from Christ.

Normally I shied away from compliments or tried to dismiss them. But this, I received. This was what my heart yearned for from a man. This was the love I had always hoped to find. As the Lord spoke to me later He said, "My love returned your love." In finding the one true love in Jesus, fulfiller of all that I desired, He provided the companion on earth for which I had dreamed.

Alan and I prayed together, prayed for our family together, spoke of what the Lord did in our day together and praised Him together. He enjoyed going to church. When I would ask him if he wanted to attend a Jesus-oriented event he would instantly say, "Yes!"

This was new to me and surprised me every time he agreed so quickly. I still am not used to it. It still makes me smile in surprise.

Yet, Satan still tried to pick at me. My own mind and pride would sometimes interfere with God's goodness. Sometimes I would think, "Wow, Alan got to live like that and then, Lord, You gave Him all that stuff! Your healing, Your Spirit..." and I would have a twinge of, "It's not fair." Then the Lord would remind me that I was only a child of twelve years when I received more of Him. I had done nothing to earn it. And as He does, He showed me a Bible verse. (Okay, you have to know this, as I'm writing, I'm thinking... "Okay, Lord, what was that verse again, I need to put it in." I reached for my Bible and it opened to that verse!!! God does this sort of stuff! He does!!! Know that He does! Believe that He does! He will do it for you if you trust Him with it. Please, trust Him with you.) The verse is Acts 11:15-17 (NLT), "Well, I began telling them the Good News, but just as I was getting started, the Holy Spirit fell on them, just as he fell on us at the beginning. Then I thought of the Lord's words when he said, 'John baptized with water, but you will be baptized with the Holy Spirit.' And since God gave these Gentiles the same gift he gave us when we believed in the Lord Jesus Christ, who was I to argue?" Who was I to argue?! I giggled with delight, knowing they too, were a little irked but had no argument because it had happened to them the same way.

People who have walked with the Lord get into a funk of pride. It is our human condition. Even these blessed disciples and those who had been with the promised Messiah felt like, “Hey, He’s giving these guys this stuff?!” That’s where I have learned that I often try to squeak myself onto the throne instead of letting Jesus sit there. My place is on my knees in front of Him and alongside everyone else on earth. His gifts are for His glory. All of our sin is equal in His eyes.

Verse eighteen goes on to say, “When the others heard this, all their objections were answered and they began praising God. They said, ‘God has also given the Gentiles the privilege of turning from sin and receiving eternal life.’” Jesus let me remember my turning away from Him, and how He fully received and forgave me when I came back. He blessed me and carried me through a life that wasn’t easy and then brought about His great glory. I never earned it. He blessed me with this story, the story of His glory.

Bitterness is a tough root to eradicate. But, I kept seeking God. Many people would feel like they could never do that—they could never forgive and get over it. The way I see it is if I wanted to go to England from where I am in Minnesota, I would not be able to do it on my own. I may be able to walk for a while, but I would never be able to make the swim across the Atlantic. I’d have to trust a pilot and a plane to get me there.

Jesus was the pilot who brought me into that plane and power of God. By His death and resurrection, I was able to fly with God and get to that place freed from pain, able to forgive and able to receive the comfort of His Holy Spirit. Even His Spirit is in this analogy. As I fly I am given pillows, blankets and water, information about where we are and how to be safe, all for my comfort and counsel while en route to my destination. Only in that way, through that from the Father, Son, and Spirit am I able to arrive to my desired destination.

Still, the Lord tests how well we are doing and trusting Him with what He has given. The tests are a good reminder of what we need to review or refresh so that it becomes part of our knowing. Our tests have our names on them. If you are being tested, it only affects you.

I was driving to an appointment. Alan and I had plans to meet up afterward. On my way, I realized I would be about ten or fifteen minutes late to meet Alan. I called him to let him know. He said he didn't want to meet me anymore, because it would be getting too late. I was furious!

I hung up my phone as I drove a section of the highway. I stepped on the gas in anger. My thoughts filled my head, "He hasn't changed; he will always be like that!" I rounded the exit ramp and came to a screeching halt at the top because of a red light. I was squeezing the steering wheel so hard my knuckles were white and I slammed on the brakes harder than needed. I looked up at the van in front of me. I read the license plate that was smack dab in front of my face. It read, 'OLORI.'

My name! My name with the Holy "O" in it! If you spend much time in the Bible, you see holy "O's" all over the place! I instantly began spouting out, "I'm sorry Lord, I'm sorry, I'm sorry! Forgive me! Please! Forgive me!" As the light turned green and I started to drive forward and make my left turn, my phone rang. It was Alan and he said he would meet me.

This is God. He interacts, He teaches, He tests, and He teaches some more. He showed me that I still had roots of bitterness and all of my anger came up with one flush and the muck backed up all over the place! He cleaned my roots out with a single license plate. He tested me and I learned to KNOW that God did a complete work and that I need to fully—I mean FULLY forgive and forget—just as He did.

I still get irritated from time to time, but believe me, that was the last of the fury. My heart has been quickened back to the place of trust as I look to the Lord and think on all of the good that He has done, just as it says in Philippians. "And now, dear brothers and sisters, one final thing. Fix your thoughts on what is true, and honorable, and right, and pure, and lovely, and admirable. Think about things that are excellent and worthy of praise.[9] Keep putting into practice all you learned and received from me—everything you heard from me and saw me doing. Then the God of peace will be with you" (Phil 4:8-9, NLT).

A new life. I was collecting the spoils just like in 2 Chronicles 20, after they showed up and sang and praised and watched God turn the enemy against themselves instead of on His people , they ran down to the site of the battle and scooped up all of the loot laying there.

Some of my loot was Alan coming home from a workout at our club and saying, "Do you want to do dance classes with me?" I loved to dance. My toe tapped to every beat. He never enjoyed dancing unless he'd had a few. He wanted to learn to waltz, fox trot, and rhumba with me. This dancing girl couldn't say yes fast enough!

We danced for months. He worked hard at exercising, dropping weight, and getting fit. His personal trainer started to warn him that running the mileage a marathoner runs, with a larger body and frame, wasn't good for his body. He told Alan he would break.

Alan kept going... and he broke. He was feeling his hamstring getting tighter. He thought he'd pulled something, but he had always just "played" that stuff out before. He eventually noticed pain in his back and had a harder time sleeping in the bed. He spent a night on the couch. Getting up the next morning, he turned a little, putting too much rotation in his back. It went.

He crawled to the bathroom. He cried and screamed. He couldn't get up. He couldn't walk. I had no way to get him around. I remembered that our church had wheelchairs for people's use. I called over quickly and asked if we could use one. My dad made the drive to get it as I stayed with Alan.

Doctor visits, x-rays and MRI's became our next months. I was loading Alan in and out of our car, loading our pre-school son into his car seat and hefting up the old steel wheelchair everywhere we went. It was taking a physical toll on me as well as emotionally. I was sad and disappointed in what I thought God had given me. "Lord, you made him new inside, you gave us a new life. Now you want me to physically care for him like this?"

It hurt. I felt hurt. But it didn't last forever. Alan started to make progress. He managed to get to crutches and then eventually walk, but with an extensive limp. After months and months of limping and epidurals for pain flair up, he decided to have surgery on the nerve that had been pinched. A piece of bone had grown over and was crushing the nerve.

The surgery took care of the pain and his limp was greatly lessened. Prayer covered that surgery and Alan sought the Lord through all of it.

Chapter 16

Jersey Shirt

We enjoyed a year of knowing and loving each other in a relationship with Jesus. Our love for each other grew and our faith in Jesus grew, too. The unity would find its place in so many surprising ways. Previously, we'd had a difference in music preference on the radio. Getting into the car that first time with Alan already in and hearing Christian praise and worship music on—and now he was enjoying it. I plopped into my car seat and said to him, "Who are you?!" He would laugh. He started listening to it at work, too, as he would come home singing one of the songs.

He had joy, I had joy, surely Jesus was double joyful. It was almost a year since we had attended the Holy Spirit conference where our marriage was fully restored. I asked Alan if he would like to go again, since it was kind of like a new one-year anniversary. Right away he said yes. We planned to celebrate and praise the Lord together for all He had done for us.

I went online to read up on who was coming to teach, looking for and hoping for another night like the year before. I couldn't really get any sense of who we should hear so I thought that we should just go on Friday night again like we did last year. I wasn't in tune with who's-who in the world of Christian speakers. My world had consisted of walking with the Lord quite alone. There was a picture of the fellow who was speaking Friday night, so I had an idea of what he would look like.

That Friday night, as Alan started to pull into the church, it was filled in the main parking lot. This church holds thousands of people. We had given ourselves fifteen to twenty minutes before the night started and it was already packed. We pulled into a section of parking much farther away, found a spot and hurried our way into the rear part of this very large building. I was ahead of Alan and I was, as Alan says, "legging it"—an English phrase for hurrying.

A woman called out loudly, "There is seating in here! The auditorium is full!" I swiftly glanced into the room she was trying to usher us into and I saw chairs and a screen. There was no way in the world I was going to miss out on the sensation of a Spirit-filled room with live speaker. I barreled passed her and it almost embarrassed Alan as he tried to keep up. We entered into the auditorium from the back upper balcony. The auditorium was full! But, in the very back of that balcony were some chairs. We sat down and Alan pointed out how I completely ignored the woman. I didn't care. I was in. The only ones behind us were children on the floor with baby dolls and toy cars. We were far, but we were in.

Just as the evening was beginning to start and people were on stage, another man came walking past swiftly, like he knew what he was doing. I looked up and saw it. Alan saw it, too. The man was wearing an orange soccer jersey just like the one Alan wore with the Minnesota Kicks in the late '70's. The man turned and went down some stairs and on the back was written "Willey" and the number nine. It was my husband's jersey! Alan sprang from his chair and almost chased him down the stairs as the man made his way to the stage. I knew. I recognized him from the picture online. He was going to be our speaker.

My knees started shaking. Under my breath I started saying, "Oh, Jesus, what are you doing?" Alan returned to his chair and said, "Did you see that?! He's wearing my jersey!" Alan was shocked and beside himself. He knew that back then, there weren't any replica jerseys made. There were t-shirts sold with the team name on them, but never player shirts or replica shirts. Still shaking, I watched the man lean into the person on stage and whisper something and then he left. I told Alan, "I think he's the speaker tonight." The man on stage then asked all of us to pray for the voting going on with the ELCA churches. The jersey guy had a prayer request and got thousands of people to pray right then. I don't think Alan and I prayed. I think we were dumbstruck.

Worship and singing started. We sang a song that we sang last year. It was Hosanna. It was the song we walked in on when we attended the year before and it was the song that started the night out. We sang and the shaking started to subside and we were peaceful again. Then it was time for the speaker. The introductions were made and in walked the jersey guy, just as I thought. There he was—wearing Alan's jersey with Alan's name and number on him. We both looked at each other, white-faced and mouths hanging open.

The jersey guy was David Housholder. David started to speak and some of the first words he said were, "If you think you know Jesus, you don't. Jesus messes with you." He didn't have to say it twice for us to remember that.

We continued to hyperventilate, shake, and sweat. Just when our pulse returned to some normality, he would turn around and the jumbo screen behind him would display a giant picture of what we were seeing—Alan's name and number written on his back. Right back to the hyperventilating, shaking, and sweating we would go.

After about two hours of the message, and being led in worship and singing, and offering praise free-form as we sang our own individual God song, Alan and I decided to make a move. Earlier, we had made our way down to the lower level to hear better, scoring some metal chairs up against a wall. As things were quieting and people were starting to leave, we saw some of our friends from church. Our pastor and his wife walked by and we told them the speaker was wearing Alan's jersey. Other friends who knew soccer had noticed it, too. They giggled and marveled at what on earth that was about.

I told Alan that he needed to go up and introduce himself to David and bless him. He had already planned to do just that, he said. As we made our way forward, passing people praying in the aisles, visiting and worshiping, we got close to the stage.

There was a lot of prayer going on. There was anointing of prayer where people were being blessed so closely by the Holy Spirit that they were going limp, and people were nearby catching them as they gently rested them to the floor. A woman who was praying over people saw Alan and asked him to catch a man as she prayed. Alan said okay. I stood and watched in amazement as Alan so readily did this. He wasn't the least bit freaked out. I myself had never experienced that type of anointing before, so it was fun to be up close and watch it happen.

It turned into catching more and more people for Alan. Alan got to the point where he said, "I am just trying to get to this guy—he's wearing my shirt!" As

Alan tells it, he says he was making more catches than Joe Mauer—a famous Minnesota Twins baseball player and catcher. The woman finally noticed Alan's insistence to stop catching people and get to the guy with his shirt. She told him okay and said, "Let me bless you." As she put her hands on him and began to pray, Alan dropped to the ground. My eyes got huge! Then she came at me, and while she was speaking my head was turned, looking down at Alan. She said, "He is a blessing, he is a blessed man of God, you are blessed, care for him." Then, *boop*, I was down.

I had been anointed by the Spirit. The strength of it to make you go limp is as gentle as being limp, but it cannot be stopped when it comes. It shares the softness of water and the strength of a wave; a combination physically and spiritually that could only be done by God. I opened my eyes and looked over and there was Alan, right beside me. I started giggling. I couldn't help myself. This was wild!

Alan heard me giggling and he said that was what made him open his eyes. The light overhead was shining right into his eyes as he squinted and tried to figure out what happened. We got up and he said again, "I just wanna get to this guy!" We staggered and giggled our way over and Alan waited as people took turns talking to the speaker.

Then it was time. Alan held out his hand, they shook, and Alan said, "I'm Alan Willey." David took a step back and said, "Are you kidding me?!" They briefly exchanged pleasantries. David told Alan how he used to go to the soccer games. He handed Alan his card and we left. We couldn't believe it and we knew God had spoken. He had spoken through a shirt. What He was saying, we didn't know. But we knew it was Him.

Chapter 17

Caught in the Current

The next day, Saturday, Alan played golf. He said it was hard to concentrate and that he told the guys what had happened. Sunday morning came and we overslept. We missed our usual church service, but I remembered that David, the jersey guy, was teaching at Hosanna, and that they had a service we could catch. We whipped around, got ready, and headed out. Hosanna was also the song that had been played and sung at the two times we went to the conference.

This was the first time we had ever been to this church. It was HUGE! There were doors numbered. Alan said it had as many doors as the Mall of America. We found a parking place fairly close to door seven. In we walked, looking at the bustle of people and the vast size of the place. We made our way to the sanctuary and walked a few steps.

The first person we saw was David! He looked as shocked to see us as we were to see him first thing among the multitudes. He grabbed Alan's hand and shook it hard and quickly introduced us to his friend who looked like he'd seen a ghost. I thought it was such an odd way to look at someone to whom you were just introduced. We said hello and we left to find some seats.

We got settled in and looked all over this spacious place that was filling up with people. After we finished singing, David came on stage. Next to him was a stool with Alan's jersey laying over it.

David began to tell a story. He started to tell the story of the jersey. We sat, hanging onto every word. He told of how he went to the soccer games as a kid on his bike, crossing what is now a busy freeway and locking his bike to the chain link fence. He told about the magnitude of the games, the crowds, and the excitement. He said that thirty years later, he had to get a jersey. He didn't know why, he just had to.

David told of the lengths it took to find a de-funked team jersey from a Minnesota soccer team that nobody even talks about anymore. He was attempting this from his home in California. He eventually decided he would have it made. He asked a friend, Laurie Bell, to make it for him and she said she couldn't because those things have copyrights and she could lose her sewing machines over it. He would need to have permission. I have since met Laurie—surprisingly, she lives in Minnesota where she runs her company, Dakota Logo. She told me that when she told David she wouldn't be able to do it, she thought, "Phew! Now he'll go away." David didn't stop.

He remembered that Don Byerly, owner of a local grocery company in Minnesota, had held ownership with the team. David said he used to bag groceries at one of those stores as a teenager, so he started looking for Don Byerly. It took him ages. David had been living in Huntington Beach, California and he was searching all over Minnesota for Don Byerly. He ended up finding Don Byerly living in California.

Don gave permission to make a shirt. David told him that it would need to be in writing and Don provided it. As Laurie told me, David came back with the permission and a choice of two names and numbers for Laurie to print on the back. One was for Ntsoelengoe, the player who had been inducted with Alan into the Hall of Fame and who had been by his side during Alan's playing career, and the other was Willey. Laurie went for the shortest name.

David had his shirt made. He said that the whole process took about two years to do and he spent about two hundred dollars doing it. My head rang with the information. Two years ago was the time I prayed desperately for God to give Alan a godly, "cool" friend who would encourage Alan and be someone Alan would admire. David was COOL! David was a man who looked at least fifteen years younger than his age. A pastor, surfer, writer, and snowboarder who wore jeans and flip-flops while he spoke and often kicked his flip-flops off. They didn't come any cooler than that. Here he was all wrapped up with Alan's name and number on him.

The other point that rang was the cost. The night that David spoke at the conference on Friday, an offering was passed. I knew I had given twenty dollars the year before. I quietly asked God this year how much He would like me to give. He said, "Two hundred dollars." Whoa, that was a lot more than last year, but since He had totally freaked me out and the speaker was wearing my last name too, I wrote the check. Now I was hearing how God even synced us in the financial part of it. David had put two hundred dollars into getting the shirt.

He went on to tell how he had made the decision of what to wear that night for the conference. He'd had his dress shirt and for whatever reason, he'd thrown the jersey into his suitcase. He started to put on the dress shirt, but knew he had to put on the jersey. He did and his wife, Wendy, said, "Are you really going to wear that?!" He told her he just had to.

As David continued to tell the story to all of us, he went on to say how at the end of the night, a man came walking up to him and introduced himself and said, “I’m Alan Willey.” The crowd listening with us all gasped. He went on to say, “It gets better,” and he tells them about how we walked into church this morning. The crowd gasps again. Then he tells them that we are here right now and he asked us to stand up. We can hardly stand because we are hearing all of this for the first time and freaking out beyond words. Then David points at Alan and says, “God has a call on your life.” He said it in front of hundreds and hundreds of people.

David reminded the people that sometimes God will ask you to do things, or you start doing something, that seems crazy. He spoke of Noah building the ark and Mrs. Noah wondering what on earth he was doing and he was saying, “I just have to.”

Alan and I halfway collapsed into our seats again. At the end of the service people came up and shook our hands. I know our heads were swirling and things were blurry.

We left stunned with the other side of the story. We went boating that afternoon and neither one of us hardly said two words to the other. The whole event was swirling and doing something...what it was, we didn’t know.

The next day David and Alan spent hours texting one another trying to figure out how everything fit, who the other was and what’s going on. I called our daughter who was working at Mt. Carmel again, two and a half hours away in northern Minnesota. I wanted to tell her what had happened and started saying, “You won’t believe this...” She interrupted me saying, “You mean about Dad’s shirt?” I blurted, “What?!”

She told me there was a huge family reunion going on at camp and the man who organized it, Luthor Nelson, co-pastored with David Housholder in Huntington Beach, California at Robinwood Church. David had called him about what had happened on Friday night. Our daughter Kristin told me that she was standing in the cafeteria while the families were lining up for the line to get their food. Luthor saw her name tag that read Kristin Willey. He asked, "By chance, do you know Alan Willey?" She exclaimed, "Yes, he's my dad!" Luthor told her the story and he told the people of Mt. Carmel, the people who had prayed for Kristin and for us as a family, the dear people who loved us and welcomed us back as a couple. They got to hear first about this amazing thing that God had just done. I was so happy for them to be a part in it, too.

That month more things happened. We went to a roadside vegetable stand. As we were walking toward the tables a beautiful, high-end convertible car came pulling in as we were crossing the road. It stopped. I looked at it at first with envy, then I tried to console myself that stuff doesn't matter—I even said in my head about the driver, "Yeah, but does he have Jesus?" As the man got out of the car with his wife and two children, I see he is wearing a t-shirt that has Bible verses on it from the book of Matthew. I am instantly struck with my judgment and the lesson just learned. I went to him and told him what I just did in my mind and how God just used him to teach me a lesson. He looked surprised and automatically defended himself and said, "I have Jesus big time! I bought the car to enjoy all of His creation!" as he stretched his arms up and out, looking at all of it.

It didn't stop: God used another shirt. That week I went grocery shopping. I saw a lovely woman wearing a pretty blue top with a nice little gathering at the chest and the color was a sapphire blue... beautiful. It was so pretty, I stopped three different times when I saw her in the store and admired it. I remembered my mom telling me that I looked good in that color.

I drove home and opened the back of my car and took out a bag of groceries. My mom came pulling into the driveway as I stood there. She hadn't stopped by in weeks. She jumped out of the car and had a small bag. She said, "I saw this and I knew you had to have it." I looked in the bag and it was that exact blue top! If ever I felt like God winked at me, it was then! What a God! He is everywhere and in everything and in every part of our lives.

Mine and Alan's true wedding anniversary was at the end of that month. We went out to dinner. In that time, Alan became fond of David and a friendship and bond developed. Alan was following him on Twitter. Alan's a techie and loves his cell phones. David would Twitter Bible verses every day. Alan would get those verses.

As we sat in our booth, Alan received a Twitter from David. Then Alan opened up a Bible application he had downloaded and began reading the Bible verse to me! I was stunned again, to be sitting there celebrating our anniversary with Alan, a new man of God, reading scripture to me! I think God likes to show off what He did, and this was definitely one of them.

After all of this had gone on, Alan told the rest of the story to our pastor. Our pastor asked if Alan would tell it at the first Sunday service of the Fall kick- off for the new year. Alan instantly said that he would. Again, I was stunned. I knew how painful it was for him to talk. I remembered how nervous he was when he had to give his acceptance speech in New York. He does a wonderful job, but he is a mess.

He wasn't a mess for this. He was happy, he had fun, and he talked for twenty-five minutes! He told all about the night of the jersey. He told them how he caught people who were being anointed by the Spirit and how he had been anointed. This was stuff a lot of people in our mostly-traditional congregation hadn't really heard about before. Alan told it honestly and humorously, and he had them glued. He was publicly stating his faith and God's works in front of a church full of people.

Quietly in my heart, I knew God was going to have me share the other side of the story. Of how God, in His glory, answered prayer, restored us, and brought miracles into our lives. I sensed He was going to have me share it at a women's retreat. After Alan spoke, there was a rally outside of the church with booths featuring classes, events, and other things the church was offering that year. A woman came walking up to me and grabbed me by the hand and stuffed a postcard into it. I held it up and read it. It was for a women's retreat that was being held in February. I nodded quietly to the Lord with a smirk on my face and in my mind told Him, "Okay."

Chapter 18

The One

February came and Alan knew what I would be doing. It was the first weekend away from him since we had reunited our marriage in Christ. As I shared with the women at the retreat about what my life had been, what I had prayed, and what God had done, I told them that now Alan is at home praying for me as I join all of them. He is no longer making it difficult for me to be around women, but is being supportive and praying for me. God did it all. And it is all to His glory that we have been allowed to live this and see Him in it. I even told them how I met Alan. I told about pinching his bum. Thankfully, they all laughed.

I had been a familiar face in the church. They never knew much about me and they seemed to think I had it made. The confessions, the truth, and the good, bad, and ugly broke down walls as women began sharing their struggles at home. A few women also began to confess their life of secretly being Spirit-filled. We had been hiding the worst and the best.

Driving home I knew I was going to have to tell my mom the truth of how we met now that many of her friends from church knew the truth. I sure didn't want her finding out from one of them—the shock of the truth would be enough. It didn't need to be compounded with the word coming from one of her esteemed saints. I got home and Alan and Sam jumped out at me from the door and tackled me to the floor and kissed me. He asked how it went and reminded me again how he was praying for me.

When I did bring myself to go to see my mom, I got to her house and my dad was in the other room. It would be easier telling one, but this was still going to be hard.

As I told her about that night and the nightclub, how I didn't think I'd see him again, that I'd been drinking, and how I'd pinched and thought it was funny and that he'd come into the place I was working the next day, she looked at me straight-faced and seriously. I could see she was thinking but not saying a word. She was just listening. When I finished, she spoke. "Lori, I could never have done that to your dad." She paused and I looked down at my feet and shook my head, and then she said, "He doesn't have anything to pinch!"

I looked up with a wide-open smile as my eyes looked back and forth on this woman, my mother, who I realized I didn't really know. I had not given her credit for being a woman or even a woman with a sense of humor! And, she is in fact married to a man with a little less in his back carriage than most. Twenty- five years! Twenty-five years I carried that lie and shame when there was no need! Oh, what we do to ourselves because of what we try to hide or protect or keep under wraps because of what we think other people would think. What we do when we don't expect understanding or compassion from someone else.

Even though I had been a woman living for Jesus all of those years, I didn't fully accept the past as His glory of redemption. Those were parts of me that had been the path He has allowed to bring me to the place where I am. The past was the part of God's glory of redemption in me *and* Alan.

Alan continued to receive requests to speak in other churches and at a men's banquet. He shared more about his soccer days, confessing infidelity, and coming to Jesus and the glory of God restoring our marriage.

One evening we were out to dinner at the same place we had celebrated our last wedding anniversary. We were with David, who was in town speaking again. I placed my leftover food into a to-go container and then tucked it into my purse. When we got back to the house I discovered that it had seeped out and spilled into my purse.

I pulled out a notebook that contained some work notes and I wanted to see what was still salvageable. I discovered notes stuck together that I had written when Alan and I were at the end of our marriage two years before. I had written what my dream husband would be like. I read aloud down the list to Alan: Someone who loves God first, someone I can pray with and will walk in the Lord with me, someone who loves the children, someone who adores me, who gets me and has a good sense of humor...and on. As I finished reading it, Alan exclaimed, "That's me!" It was! Again, God showed what wonderful things He did.

Next, the Lord called me to volunteer for leadership in a Bible study with over 150 women. This was not me. I never lead. I had only served in Sunday school with preschoolers. Somehow, God took me and made me able to speak and encourage, and bring humor and sweetness from Him to all of those ladies. We did prayer ministry and the Lord was pouring out His love on them, giving them hope, healing, and joy. The Lord let me find joy in it, just like Alan did telling about Jesus in his life.

As I did this study, I wrote the homework that coincided with Beth Moore's DVD series *The Inheritance.* This study showed me in Psalm 16:5, "The lines have fallen for me in pleasant places, indeed I have a beautiful inheritance" (ESV). As I studied this, knowing that lots were cast as the tribes of Israel received their portion for their life, God was in control of how those lots fell. Nothing was chance. Another part of the study emphasized how God is our portion and we are His.

While working on the study, a song played on the radio by the Turtles, "So Happy Together," written by Gary Bonner and Alan Gordon in 1967. It totally went with our study! Some of the lyrics are, "No matter how they tossed the dice it had to be, the only one for you is Me and you for Me, so happy together." I had re-thought the "me" part to being God as "Me."

There it was, our inheritance study summed up in a song. Not even one written to be a Christian song. I actually played it at one of our study nights! As I was writing our story about my life in search of love and remembered how I sat in the soccer stadium, alone with our daughter listening to this very song by this very band and the loneliness I had; it came back to me that I used this song in our study. It had the whole new meaning of that love being God. I can see God was there with me, in that time in the stadium; though I was lonely, I wasn't alone. God had left a trail of Him—in every part of my life—of love, as I found Him to be the perfect love.

He magnified it in front of me. He showed me that truth with the very first date with a boy who sold t-shirts at the stadium where I was rejected by him. Where at the stadium, another boy was chaining his bike to the fence to watch a player he enjoyed and would someday become the platform that brought glory to God from the glory days of soccer by wearing a jersey. Where in that stadium, the man I would marry was a star playing on a field as God was preparing the fields of our lives. When I went through life with that man, holding fast to faith and hope and learning how to love Jesus first, Jesus was there. He showed Himself boldly in that very soccer shirt on a man hand-picked by God. He moved Alan into a place of publicly proclaiming his faith and allowing our story to be heard. He taught me through a shirt, and blessed me with a shirt.

He's personal, He knows your name, and He's got your number. God moves in our lives, leaving messages of His presence. A memory that is strong has meaning. It has Him in it somehow, someway.

I wondered why my memories of my brother were so strong when he stepped in and helped me back then. Later, his marriage was to suffer and almost end. It looked hopeless, but he said, "If God can heal your marriage, He can heal mine, too." I was able to pray for my brother, encourage my brother, and love my brother through Jesus. It was my turn to help him in his time of struggle and I had been given the tools for how to faithfully hope. God was there and brought healing to his marriage at that time, too. God did it for them. And I believe the Lord allowed me to comfort my brother as he had comforted me so long ago.

New Year's Eve of this year, Alan and I and our son went to stay with family in Iowa. The family who had prayed for us with faces to the ground continued to be dear to us. As the evening rolled along, we read scripture all together and discussed it, as was often what they did from their days in *L'abri.* Alan was engrossed. I didn't fidget for fear he was uncomfortable or uninterested like before when we would gather.

Then we pushed back the furniture and rolled up the rug and we danced until midnight. We barn danced, Scottish line-danced, and more. There was the couple—my cousin and his wife—who shared a kiss that tasted of sweet champagne after they were newly married, as they stopped at our house. It had sparked the desire that I longed to have such a marriage so centered on Christ and now, Alan and I, equally grounded on Jesus, linked arms with them and twirled each other about. The joy and jubilation continued to be shown as God touched each desire, showing me He knew and knows. And I think Alan danced the hardest.

Blessings continue to come. By the efforts of his daughter, Andrea, in England, communication began with Alan this year which has now brought a reconnection with his oldest son, Graeme. His first wife requested Alan as a friend on Facebook© and now they are friends. Nothing is impossible with God.

The Lord, in our life, was sometimes subtle and sometimes bold. He was in shirts, songs, sacks of groceries, friends, family, strangers, snow, fields, phone calls, His spoken or written Word, nudges, notebooks, license plates, successes, losses, and blessings. His love was and is and will always be right there. We only need to reach out our hand to His.

"But even so, you love me! You are holding my right hand! You will keep on guiding me all my life with your wisdom and counsel, and afterwards receive me into the glories of heaven!" (Psalms 73: 23-24, TLB).

We see this life as one leading to our eternal life. We see how we are still here, as the teammate who was alongside Alan for those special times is no longer on earth. What God has for us here is Him everywhere, getting to know Him until we may fully know His glories in heaven.

Our home that we have lived in for the last fourteen years—sits modestly and only blocks away from where I grew up—but I see how far the Lord has moved us spiritually in our lives with Him. Our home backs up to a public soccer field. Children, men, and women play soccer as we quietly watch from our windows—unknown to them that a soccer legend is only feet away. But, much bigger is God. Right there. With them. He loves them, He sent Jesus for them and He is there on that field and knows the fields of His plans for them and for all of us, and as Mary said, "But, being the gentleman that He is, we need to ask." We need to ask Him to forgive the days of our pasts, believe what He did for us on the cross and what He will do for us in the same power He used rising from the grave, and start living our lives on the field for His glory.

As I look back even on this story, in the second paragraph I wrote: "I imagined my prince to be completely in love with me. He would be jealous of my attentions. He would protect me from other's advances. He would be strong and carry me in his arms in play and romance. He would be thoughtful and always there for me and would never want to leave me. He would provide for me, laugh with me and comfort me. We would do everything together for the rest of our lives." It is our Lord. He's the One.

For richer, for poorer, for better for worse, in sickness and in health, He is the One and He is our true love. He's always faithful and never forsakes. He listens, forgives, answers, shields, provides, comforts, delivers, heals, restores, uplifts, defends, conquers, loves, and waits for you. No person can fulfill that. Our Savior is the only one. His story is an ever-after story. His glory is unending.

Suggested Reading.

The Blackberry Bush by David Housholder and published by Summerside Press. David, the jersey guy, wrote *The Blackberry Bush* following our encounter the night he wore Alan's jersey. The encounter changed him, too. He began seeing the backstory of what brought us together; each piece fitting into a bigger plan. David's fictional story is a treasure hunt through the backstory of Josh and Kati. At the end of the book he has written questions to consider, helping you discover your own backstory.

The Family Blessing by Rolf Garborg and published by Summerside Press. This book will change the way you do family and life. A blessing made anywhere and anytime in life brings about beautiful things.

Alan Willey #9 with the Minnesota Kicks.
Photo by Brian Quarstad insidemnsoccer.com

Alan heading the ball at the Met Stadium Bloomington, MN

Our Wedding Day

Praying with Sam in the Prayer Chapel at Mt. Carmel Alexandria, MN

Artist recreation by Bruce Peterson brpart58@yahoo.com

A Family: Kristin, Sam, Alan and Kendra

David Housholder wearing his jersey with his wife, Wendy.
Huntington Beach, CA Photo by Lindsey Trego

Free to praise God together. Alan, Me and Sam at Breaker's East Destin, FL